U0063154

剑桥KET考试
听力通关周计划

金利 / 编著

化学工业出版社
· 北京 ·

图书在版编目（CIP）数据

剑桥KET考试听力通关周计划/金利编著.—北京：
化学工业出版社，2024.4
（剑桥KET考试通关周计划）
ISBN 978-7-122-45250-4

Ⅰ.①剑… Ⅱ.①金… Ⅲ.①英语水平考试–听说教
学–自学参考资料 Ⅳ.①H319.9

中国国家版本馆CIP数据核字（2024）第055501号

责任编辑：马小桐 马 骄 加工编辑：温建斌 装帧设计：张 辉
责任校对：刘 一 版式设计：梧桐影

出版发行：化学工业出版社
　　　　　（北京市东城区青年湖南街13号 邮政编码100011）
印 　 装：河北京平诚乾印刷有限公司
787mm×1092mm 1/16 印张10½ 字数187千字
2024年6月北京第1版第1次印刷

购书咨询：010-64518888 售后服务：010-64518899
网 　 址：http://www.cip.com.cn
凡购买本书，如有缺损质量问题，本社销售中心负责调换。

定 　 价：49.90元 版权所有 违者必究

前言

《剑桥KET考试听力通关周计划》一书写给正在备考剑桥A2 Key(KET)听力考试的考生。我们深知准备听力考试需要一定的时间规划、思路点拨、考点锦囊以及充分练习。因此，本书采用讲解与规划相结合的学习方法，将这些要素有机地结合在一起，确保考生顺利通关。

⏱ KET考试听力通关 = **合理的时间规划 + 思路点拨 + 考点锦囊 + 每周一练**

★ 8周学习规划

按周规划好学习内容，跟着规划学，易坚持，更高效。

本书学习内容以周为单位，从考试内容入手，为考生规划好要学习和练习的内容，跟着规划走，利用碎片化时间来学习，用时少，效率高。

◇ 【周目标】每周开启学习前，了解本周学习目标。

◇ 【周中学】每周周中学习考试核心备考知识，掌握答题思路，积累考试词句。

◇ 【周末练】周六或周日，集中演练本周所学。

一周内容，以目标为导向，学练结合，知识掌握更加扎实。

★ 思路点拨 + 考点锦囊

考题呈现，剖析答题思路，分享KET听力锦囊，答题更容易。

在每周学习中，针对考试中的考题题型，本书都给出了答题的思路以及窍门（如先读题、划出关键词等）；此外，本书还针对每种题型，给出与主题相关的单词、句型或核心考点。

本书旨在帮助考生建立答题思维，而非死记硬背。有思路，有方法，有词句积累，考场答题更从容。

★ 每周一练 + 全真模拟

多样化题型操练本周所学，学后巩固练习，知识掌握更加扎实。

本书的练习题包括各种多样化的题型，如选词填空、词句匹配、听音选图、听音填表、听音判断正误等，多维度操练所学内容，进一步夯实所学，打好基础，帮助考生有效备考。

通过每周一练和全真模拟题，考生将能够熟悉各种考试题型，锻炼听力基础能力，并在实践中提高应对考试的信心。

总之，本书致力于为考生提供全面而高效的学习资源，让考生在备考剑桥A2 Key (KET) 听力考试时更有信心、更具备竞争力。希望通过本书的学习，考生能够顺利通过考试，实现自己的考试目标。

目录

Week 3　短对话图片单选题

Week 4　独白摘要题

熟悉考试

第1周目标

考试模块	时间	主题	内容	
Listening	Day 1	考试概述	考试要求及评分标准	☐
	Day 2	备考贴士	熟悉答题卡、备考建议等	☐
	Day 3	短对话图片单选题	题型详解、答题技巧、样题举例	☐
	Day 4	独白摘要题	题型详解、答题技巧、样题举例	☐
	Day 5	长对话单选题	题型详解、答题技巧、样题举例	☐
	Day 6	短对话/独白单选题	题型详解、答题技巧、样题举例	☐
	Day 7	信息匹配题	题型详解、答题技巧、样题举例	☐

Day 1　考试概述

 考试介绍

剑桥英语五级证书考试，即Main Suite Examinations (MSE)，为英国剑桥大学考试委员会所设计的英语作为外国语的五级系列考试。

A2 Key for Schools为五级考试中的第一级，即更名前的"KET青少版"考试。该考试对应欧洲语言共同参考框架（CEFR）的A2级别。通过A2 Key for Schools考试的考生能够达到以下水平。

➤ 能够理解并运用基础词组和表达。

➤ 能够理解简单的英语文本。

➤ 能够用英语进行自我介绍并回答有关个人详细信息的基本问题。

➤ 在熟悉的情景中，使用英语进行沟通。

➤ 理解简短的通知和简单的口头指示，可以书写简短的便条。

其中，听力部分是A2 Key for Schools的第二套试卷（第一套试卷为"阅读和写作"）。

✓ 听力考题分为5个部分，共计25小题。

✓ 每段录音内容读两遍。

✓ 整体考试时长为30分钟，其中包括6分钟的填涂答题卡时间。

✓ 分值为25分，占A2 Key for Schools考试总分值的25%。

🎧 题型及分值

听力部分分为5个部分，主要任务如下。

➤ 回答短篇听力文本的多道选择题。

➤ 在听一个人讲话（独白）的同时填写表格上的遗漏单词。

➤ 在听短文和长文的同时回答多道选择题。

➤ 根据说话者所说的内容，匹配信息、人员或活动的列表。

听力5种题型及具体分值比例如下。

Part 部分	Task Types 【题型】	Sample 样例截图	Number of Questions 题目数量	Number of Marks 分数
Part 1	3-option multiple choice 听5组短对话，选出一张符合问题的图片		5	5

Part 部分	Task Types 【题型】	Sample 样例截图	Number of Questions 题目数量	Number of Marks 分数
Part 2	Gap fill 听1段独白，填写表格		5	5
Part 3	3-option multiple choice 听1组长对话，选择一个恰当选项		5	5
Part 4	3-option multiple choice 听5组对话或独白，选择一个恰当选项		5	5
Part 5	Matching 听1组长对话，进行8选5匹配		5	5
总计			25	25

🎧 评分标准

听力部分共计25题，每题1分，满分25分。根据剑桥考试计分规则，A2 Key for Schools四部分（阅读、写作、听力、口语）各个部分的计分成绩总分是150分，综合成绩是将所有单项分数相加除以四计算得出。其中听力部分的25分折合成150分的计分分值如下。

听力部分卷面分数	剑桥考试标准分数	CEFR级别
25	150	Level B1+
23	140	Level B1
17	120	Level A2
11	100	Level A1
6	82*	—

* A2 Key for Schools考试报告的**最低分数**

Day 2 备考贴士

熟悉答题卡

听力考试时长一共为30分钟，其中有6分钟为填涂答题卡的时间，填涂答题卡需使用B或HB铅笔。

1. 考生的基本个人信息在答题卡中已打印好，考生需要核对个人信息，如果信息正确无误，将自己姓名全拼抄写到【Candidate Signature】框内即可（姓名的拼音需**全部大写**）。

2. 答题卡具体填涂说明。

> 选择题（Part 1，Part 3，Part 4，Part 5），将对应选项圆圈涂满、涂黑。

> Part 2书写答案时，**全部字母都需要大写**。

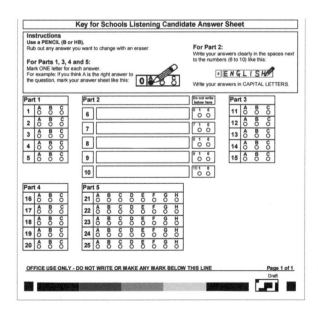

🎧 备考建议

在准备听力部分时，需要注意以下几点。

考试进行中

➤ 在听力考试过程中，利用任何停顿时间来阅读题目说明和问题。

➤ 每段录音会播放两次，尝试在第一次听的时候回答问题，然后用第二次听来检查答案，并填写第一次没有听到的答案。

➤ 记录答案时，可尝试使用一些简写（比如阿拉伯数字、缩写等），最后6分钟时，再将答案补充完整。

➤ 即便答题过程中无法确定正确答案，也要回答所有问题。

平时积累

➤ 多样化听力材料磨耳朵：可以选择一些难度适宜的新闻、广播、电影、动画、电视节目等材料，进行听力训练，比如朗读、跟读、背诵、挖空练习等。

➤ 主题词汇积累：按照主题分类记忆单词，如数字、运动、活动、人物描述等，都是听力中经常考到的主题。

🎧 考试说明录音

听力考试开始时，会播放一段有关"考试说明"的录音，在备考时可以提前熟悉。

There are five parts to the test. You will hear each piece twice.
测试有五个部分，每一段录音播放两遍。

We will now stop for a moment.
Please ask any questions now because you must NOT speak during the test.
我们现在停一下。有问题请现在提问，考试期间不允许说话。

通用"考试说明"录音播放完后，接下来会播放听力五个部分的录音。

【Part 1】

Now look at the instructions for Part 1. 现在看第一部分的考试说明。
Pause 05″ 停顿5秒
For each question, choose the correct picture. 给每一个问题选择正确的答案。
Pause 02″ 停顿2秒

Look at question one. 看问题1。

Now listen again. 现在再听一遍。

That is the end of Part 1. 第一部分到此结束。

【 Part 2 】

Now look at Part 2. 现在看第二部分。

For each question, write the correct answer in the gap. Write one word or a number or a date or a time. 针对每个问题，在空白处写下正确的答案。写一个单词或数字或日期或时间。

Look at Questions 6-10 now. You have 10 seconds. 现在看问题6～10。你有10秒的时间。

Now listen again. 现在再听一遍。

That is the end of Part 2. 第二部分到此结束。

【 Part 3 】

Now look at Part 3. 现在看第三部分。

For each question, choose the correct answer. 给每一个问题选择正确的答案。

Look at Questions 11-15 now. You have 20 seconds. 现在看问题11～15。你有20秒的时间。

Now listen again. 现在再听一遍。

That is the end of Part 3. 第三部分到此结束。

【 Part 4 】

Now look at Part 4. 现在看第四部分。

For each question, choose the correct answer. 给每一个问题选择正确的答案。

Now listen again. 现在再听一遍。

That is the end of Part 4. 第四部分到此结束。

【 Part 5 】

Now look at Part 5. 现在看第五部分。

For each question, choose the correct answer. 给每一个问题选择正确的答案。

Look at Questions 21-25 now. You have 15 seconds. 现在看问题21～25。你有15秒的时间。

Now listen again. 现在再听一遍。

That is the end of Part 5. 第五部分到此结束。

【结语】

> *You now have 6 minutes to write your answers on the answer sheet.* 现在你有6分钟的时间在答题纸上写下答案。
> *You have one more minute.* 你还有一分钟。
> *That is the end of the test.* 测试到此结束。

Day 3 短对话图片单选题

 题型分析

【**题型**】短对话图片单选题，三选一

【**题量**】5题

【**内容**】录音：五段短对话录音，长度在30～60词，每段录音播放两遍

卷面：每道题有一个问题，三个图片选项

【**要求**】听对话，根据录音以及题干，选出符合要求的图片

【**样例**】

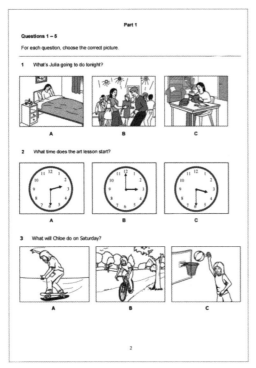

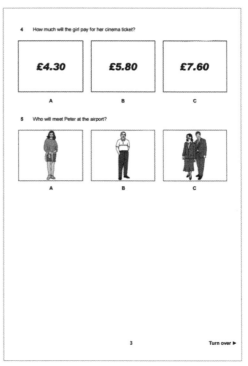

答题技巧

核心考点

✓ 考查考生抓取关键细节信息的能力。

✓ 关键信息涉及事件、日期、价格、任务、地点等。

答题步骤

针对每道题，考生答题步骤如下。

1. 阅读题干，明确问题及关键信息，便于在听的过程中进行关键信息的抓取。

2. 观察三个选项的三张图片，寻找它们之间的区别，并思考对应图片的英文表达是什么。

3. 听第一遍录音，根据前面找到的关键信息，锁定录音信息，选出答案。

4. 听第二遍录音，检查答案是否正确。

注意事项

1. 考题中几乎每幅图片都会在对话中被提到，切勿听见什么就选什么，要看清问题，然后根据图片对关键词进行判断。

2. 听音过程中需要不断辨别干扰选项，完整听完对话后再做选择。

样题解析

For each question, choose the correct picture.

How much will the girl pay for her cinema ticket?

£4.30	£5.80	£7.60
A	B	C

解析

Step 1:【审题目，找关键】

1. **题干**How much will the girl pay for her cinema ticket?

   - 关键信息：人物—the girl；事物—cinema ticket

   - 题干翻译：这个女孩要付多少钱买电影票？

2. **选项**

   - 图片A：4.30英镑—four pounds thirty

   - 图片B：5.80英镑—five pounds eighty

   - 图片C：7.60英镑—seven pounds sixty

Step 2:【听录音，选答案】

1. **听力原文**

   M: Would you like to see a film this evening?

   F: How much are the tickets? I haven't got much money this week.

   M: All tickets tonight are four pounds thirty for students like us. Usually they're five pounds eighty.

   F: Let's go then. I've got seven pounds sixty to spend. We can have a coffee afterwards.

2. **选择答案**

   - 首先出现选项A，four pounds thirty。女生询问票价，男生提到 "All tickets tonight are four pounds thirty for students like us."，即 "对于像我们这样的学生来说，今天晚上的票价都是4.30英镑"。

   - 其次出现选项B，five pounds eighty。男生除了提到学生票价之外，后面还提及 "Usually they're five pounds eighty."。根据此句可知，平时的电影票票价为5.80英镑。

   - 最后出现选项C，seven pounds sixty。女生提到 "I've got seven pounds sixty to spend."，即 "我有7.60英镑可以花"。

   - 根据以上信息，再结合题干，可知女孩购买电影票应是 "学生票" 的价格，即4.30英镑，故本题选A。

【Answer key】A

Day 4　独白摘要题

🎧 题型分析

【题型】摘要填空题，每空一词

【题量】5题

【内容】录音：一段长独白，长度在150～170词，录音播放两遍

卷面：有一句背景提要，一张待完善的信息摘要图表

【要求】听一段长独白，根据录音填写空缺的内容

【样例】

Part 2

Questions 6 – 10

For each question, write the correct answer in the gap. Write **one word** or **a number** or **a date** or **a time**.

You will hear a teacher telling students about a school camping trip.

School Camping Trip

Cost of trip:	£39.00
Give money to:	(6) Mrs _____
Day of return:	(7) _____
Time to arrive at school:	(8) _____ a.m.
Travel by:	(9) _____
Bring:	(10) _____

🎧 答题技巧

核心考点

✓ 考查考生辨别、记录特定细节信息的能力以及词汇的拼写能力。

✓ 关键信息涉及价格、日期、时间、名字、电话号码、地点或其他一些关键词等。

答题步骤

1. 阅读图表上方的文本，以了解对话进行的场所或涉及的主题。

2. 阅读图表的内容，以确定每空需要填写的信息类型，比如人名、日期、时间、交通工具等。

3. 听第一遍录音，考生将所听到的细节信息记录下来。

4. 听第二遍录音，查漏补缺，完成所有题目，并进行检查，注意拼写正确。

注意事项

1. 人名、地名等信息通常会在录音中逐个字母拼读出来，考生要留意其拼写。

2. 独白中常会出现一些干扰项，这些干扰项通常会伴随某些转折词或否定词一起出现，比如instead of、can't、not、however、but等，听到这些词时要特别注意转折后面的信息。

 样题解析

For each question, write the correct answer in the gap. Write one word or a number or a date or a time. Look at Questions 6–10 now. You have 10 seconds.

You will hear a teacher telling students about a school camping trip.

School Camping Trip	
Cost of trip:	£39.00
Give money to:	(6) Mrs _____
Day of return:	(7) _____
Time to arrive at school:	(8) _____ a.m.
Travel by:	(9) _____
Bring:	(10) _____

解析

Step 1:【审题目，找关键】

1. **文本** You will hear a teacher telling students about a school camping trip.

  • 关键信息：主题—a school camping trip（一次学校露营）

  • 题干翻译：你会听到一位老师告诉学生关于学校露营的事。

2. **图表**

(6) Give money to—把钱交给，Mrs—夫人；结合两点，此处要填入"**姓氏**"。

(7) Day of return——返程日期；此空要填入"**日期**"。

(8) Time to arrive at school——到达学校的时间；此空要填入"**时间**"。

(9) Travel by——乘坐；此空要填入"**交通工具**"。

(10) Bring——携带；此空要填入"**物品**"。

Step 2:【听录音，填答案】

1. 听力原文

M: Morning everyone. I hope you're all looking forward to our camping trip next week. Please remember that now we are staying an extra day. The trip costs thirty nine pounds, not thirty four. (6)You need to give your money to our new school secretary by the end of the week. Her name is Mrs Fairford. That's F A I R F O R D. Please go to see her soon.

As you know, (7)we are leaving on Tuesday but we're returning on Friday instead of Thursday. (8)Now——you must get to school for half past seven on Tuesday because we'll leave at a quarter to eight and we can't wait for anyone.

(9)We usually go by coach on school trips but because the campsite is near a station, we're going to go by train for a change. (10)You don't need to bring tents or anything like that, but you will need boots. We will do lots of walking by rivers so don't bring trainers because your feet will get wet. Is that clear to everyone?

2. 填入答案

(6) 根据材料中的信息"You need to give your money to... Her name is Mrs Fairford"可知，空格处应填<u>FAIRFORD</u>。

(7) 在材料中会听到三个时间点："leaving on Tuesday"、"returning on Friday"、"instead of Thursday"。要抓住关键词"return"，"instead of"是"而不是"的意思，所以排除"Thursday"，应填入<u>FRIDAY</u>。

(8) 材料中会听到两个相关的时间点："get to school for half past seven"和"leave at a quarter to eight"。图表中的"arrive at school"就等同于材料中的"get to school"，即"到达学校"，故应填入"half past seven"对应的<u>7:30</u>。

(9) 材料中会听到两种交通方式："go by coach on school trips"和"go by train for a change"。很多考生听到"usually go by coach"时，会误以为是"by coach"，注意本句中的转折词"but"，后面才是说话者真正的意图，露营地靠近火车站，所以我们要去坐火车，所以应填写<u>TRAIN</u>。

(10) 材料中提到两种物品，"tents"和"boots"，注意关于"tents"前面说的是"You don't need to bring"，所以"tents"是不需要的；而"boots"前面是"but you will need"，也就是所需要的，故填入<u>BOOTS</u>。

Day 5　长对话单选题

 题型分析

【题型】文字选择题，三选一

【题量】5题

【内容】录音：一段非正式长对话，长度在160～190词，录音播放两遍

卷面：一句背景提要；每道题有题干和三个文本选项

【要求】听一段长对话，根据录音选出正确的答案

【样例】

Part 3

Questions 11 – 15

For each question, choose the correct answer.

You will hear Annie talking to her friend Tony about a film she saw.

11 Annie saw a film at

    A two o'clock.

    B quarter past three.

    C half past five.

12 The film was about

    A a sports star.

    B some animals.

    C history.

13 Annie thought the film

    A was too long.

    B wasn't very interesting.

    C needed better actors.

答题技巧

核心考点

- ✓ 考查考生听日常对话，从中获取细节信息的能力。
- ✓ 题目主要考查两位说话者的观点、态度、意见等。

答题步骤

1. 阅读并收听题目上方的说明，以明确对话的背景（人物关系和话题内容）。

2. 快速浏览每道题目题干及选项信息，初步了解答题关键点，便于在听音过程中重点关注。

3. 听第一遍录音，考生应抓住要点，为每个问题选择最佳答案。

4. 听第二遍录音，查漏补缺，完成所有题目，检查已选择的答案是否正确。

注意事项

1. 每道题的错误选项通常也会在录音中出现，考生需注意辨别正确信息。

2. 录音中出现的每一个问句，一般可能是下一题的开始，接下来就可能是答案所在的部分，注意做题的节奏。

3. 通常情况，5道题目是符合顺序出题原则的，即5道题目的信息会依次出现在录音中。

 样题解析

Questions 11 – 15

For each question, choose the correct answer.

You will hear Annie talking to her friend Tony about a film she saw.

11 Annie saw a film at

    A two o'clock.   **B** quarter past three.   **C** half past five.

12 The film was about

    A a sports star.   **B** some animals.   **C** history.

13 Annie thought the film

    A was too long.   **B** wasn't very interesting.   **C** needed better actors.

14 Annie's favourite film

    A makes her laugh.   **B** is a true story.   **C** is very exciting.

15 Annie prefers to watch films

    A at a cinema.   **B** on her laptop.   **C** on TV.

解析

Step 1:【审题目，找关键】

1. **背景信息** You will hear **Annie** talking to her **friend Tony** about a **film** she saw.

   - 关键信息：人物—Annie和Tony；人物关系—friend；对话主题—film

   - 文本翻译：你会听到安妮和她的朋友托尼谈论她看过的一部电影。

2. **题干及选项**

   (11) [题干] Annie saw a film **at**—安妮在_____（几点）看电影

   [选项] A two o'clock—两点钟；B quarter past three—三点一刻；C half past five—五点半

   [答案]选择"**安妮看电影的时间**"。

   (12) [题干] The film was **about**—这部电影是关于_____

   [选项] A a sports star—一个运动明星；B some animals——一些动物；C history—历史

   [答案]选择"**电影的主题**"。

   (13) [题干] Annie **thought** the film—安妮认为这部电影_____

   [选项] A was too long—太长了；B wasn't very interesting—不是很有趣；C needed better actors—需要更好的演员

   [答案]选择"**安妮对电影的看法**"。

   (14) [题干] Annie's **favourite film**—安妮最喜欢的电影_____

   [选项] A makes her laugh—让她大笑；B is a true story—是一个真实的故事；C is very exciting—是令人非常兴奋的

   [答案]选择"**安妮最喜欢的电影是什么样的**"。

   (15) [题干] Annie **prefers** to watch films—安妮喜欢看电影（的方式）_____

   [选项] A at a cinema—在电影院；B on her laptop—用她的笔记本；C on TV—在电视上

   [答案]选择"**安妮喜欢看电影的方式**"。

Step 2:【听录音，填答案】

1. 听力原文

M: Annie! I tried to phone you on Saturday afternoon, but your phone was off.

F: Sorry, Tony! I was at home all morning and in the evening.

M: Oh, so what did you do on Saturday?

F: I went to see a film actually. But before that I was at the shops for about two hours. [11]Then I went to the cinema for the 3:15 show and I didn't come out until half past five.

M: What was the film?

F: [12]An old one from many years ago called *The Black Lions*. It's the story of a top basketball player.

M: Did you enjoy it?

F: [13]Actually, it's an interesting story, but it's a shame there are no really good actors in it. Anyway, it's not too long!

M: Don't you prefer funny films?

F: [14]Well, my favourite film ever is *Bird Boy*, which actually isn't funny and has nothing amazing in it. But the reason I love it is because it all really happened.

M: Oh. I haven't seen it.

F: I've only seen it on TV. [15]I think it's best to see films on a big cinema screen, but I usually just watch them on my laptop at home.

M: Me too.

2. 选择答案

(11) 对话中并未明确听到包含when的问题。但根据顺序出题原则，当听到Annie说"I went to see a film actually."时，考生需注意后面的信息。根据"I went to the cinema for the 3:15 show"可知，Annie是看3:15的电影，"went to the cinema"就表示"saw a film"，故应选择"quarter past three"，即选项B。选项C"half past five"也在对话中提到，"I didn't come out until half past five."。此处的是电影结束的时间，可排除。

(12) 当听到问句"What was the film?"时，需注意，接下来要讨论的就是本题所问的"是什么电影"。答语中提到"It's the story of a top basketball player."，其中"a top basketball player"表示"顶尖的篮球运动员"，属于选项A"a sports star（体育

明星）"，故正确答案为A。上一句中虽然提到了"*The Black Lions*"，看似是和animals相关，但注意前面的"called"，此处是说该电影的名称，排除选项B。

(13) 当听到问句"Did you enjoy it?"时，要注意，后面的答语就是Annie对电影的看法。根据Annie的回答，Annie先说"it's an interesting story"，故可排除选项B。后面Annie又说"but it's a shame there are no really good actors in it."，即"可惜的是没有什么真正的好演员"，符合选项C "needed better actors"。最后Annie说"Anyway, it's not too long."，该说法和A项"too long"相反。所以正确答案为C。

(14) Annie在回答"Don't you prefer funny films?"时，提到"my favourite film"，即"我最喜欢的电影"，在描述时，Annie提到"isn't funny and has nothing amazing in it"，根据"isn't funny"和"nothing amazing"可排除选项A和C。接下来Annie提到"But the reason I love it is because it all really happened"，即"我喜欢这部电影是因为它都是真实发生的"，"really happened"和选项B "a true story"表达意思相同，故正确答案为B。

(15) Annie在对话中提到"I think it's best to see films on a big cinema screen."。根据best可知"on a big cinema screen（在电影院的大屏幕上）"是Annie最喜欢的看电影的方式，"on a big cinema screen"实际就指选项A的"at a cinema"。

Day 6　短对话/独白单选题

 题型分析

【题型】文字选择题，三选一

【题量】5题

【内容】录音：五段短对话或独白，每段长度在40～60词，每段录音播放两遍

　　　　卷面：每道题有一句背景提要，一道问题和三个文本选项

【要求】听五段短对话或独白，根据录音选出正确的答案

【样例】

Part 4

Questions 16 – 20

For each question, choose the correct answer.

16 You will hear a teacher talking to her class.
    What does the teacher want her class to do?

    A work more quickly

    B make less noise

    C help each other more

17 You will hear two friends talking about their day.
    What have they just done?

    A They've been to a concert.

    B They've had a meal.

    C They've played a sport.

18 You will hear a teacher talking to one of his students called Sarah.
    Why must Sarah do her homework again?

    A She made too many mistakes.

    B She did the wrong work.

    C She forgot to do some of it.

19 You will hear a girl, Lara, talking about shopping.
    Why did Lara buy the bag?

    A The size was right.

    B The price was right.

    C The colour was right.

答题技巧

核心考点

✓ 考查考生听日常对话或独白，抓住每段对话或独白的要点或主题的能力。

✓ 题目主要考查两位说话者的观点、态度、意见等。

答题步骤

1. 考生应先阅读题干信息，明确独白或对话中将出现的人物和关键信息，如题干中的特殊疑问句，三个选项的不同点等。

2. 听第一遍录音，考生应听取主旨大意，记录关键词，选出最佳答案。

3. 听第二遍录音，考生应检查已选择的答案是否正确。

注意事项

1. 每段录音会连续播放两遍。

2. 注意当出现转折连词时，通常后面是需要重点关注的内容。

3. 正确答案通常不会直截了当地在音频中出现，而是会间接地被说话者表达出来。注意平时对同义表达的积累。

 样题解析

Questions 16 – 20

For each question, choose the correct answer.

You will hear a teacher talking to one of his students called Sarah.

Why must Sarah do her homework again?

A She made too many mistakes.

B She did the wrong work.

C She forgot to do some of it.

解析

Step 1:【审题目，找关键】

1. **背景信息** You will hear a **teacher talking to** one of his students called **Sarah**.

   - 关键信息：人物—teacher和Sarah；事件—talking to Sarah

   - 文本翻译：你会听到一位老师和他的学生莎拉在讲话。

2. **题干** Why must **Sarah do her homework again**?

   - 关键信息：人物—Sarah；事件—do homework again；问题—why

   - 文本翻译：为什么莎拉必须要重新写作业？

3. **选项**

   - 选项A：She made too many mistakes.（她错误太多。）

   - 选项B：She did the wrong work.（她做错了作业。）

   - 选项C：She forgot to do some of it.（她忘了做一部分作业。）

Step 2:【听录音，选答案】

1. 听力原文

M: I'm afraid you need to do this maths homework again, Sarah.

F: Oh no! Didn't I finish it, Mr Hall? I'm sure I did! So—are some of my answers incorrect?

M: Not at all. You understood my lesson perfectly—but I told you to do exercise two on page six, not page sixteen!

F: Oh dear—I must be much more careful!

2. 选择答案

- 在对话第一句，老师就提到需要学生Sarah重新做数学作业，Sarah接下来用了疑问句来回复老师，第一个疑问句是 "Didn't I finish it?（难道我没有完成吗？）" 该疑问句与选项C表达的含义接近；第二个疑问句是 "So-are some of my answers incorrect?（我的答案是有一些错误吗？）" 该疑问句中的 "incorrect" 与选项A中的 "mistakes" 表述相同。针对以上两个疑问，老师的回复是 "Not at all."，所以选项A和C都可排除。

- 老师的回复中用到了转折连词but，后面表述的是让Sarah重新做作业的真正原因 "but I told you to do exercise two on page six, not page sixteen"，即 "我告诉你做第6页的练习2，不是16页的"，老师言下之意是学生没有做对作业，所以应选择B。

【Answer key】B

Day 7　信息匹配题

 题型分析

【题型】文字选择题，三选一

【题量】5题

【内容】录音：一段长对话，长度在160~180词，录音播放两遍

卷面：一句背景提要，一个整体问题和两列文本信息

【要求】听一段长对话，根据录音匹配左右两组词汇，每组词汇属于同一主题

【样例】

Part 5

Questions 21 – 25

For each question, choose the correct answer.

You will hear Julia talking to her mother about a school fashion show.
What will each person help with?

Example:

0   Julia   D

People		**Help with**	
21	Anton	**A**	clothes
22	Emma	**B**	food
23	Karl	**C**	lights
24	Sarah	**D**	make-up
25	George	**E**	music
		F	photographs
		G	posters
		H	tickets

🎧 **答题技巧**

核心考点

✓ 考查考生听熟人之间的日常对话，从中提取细节信息，并对相似信息进行辨析以及准确匹配的能力。

✓ 题目通常考查人物、物品、时间、事件、活动、地点等的信息匹配。

答题步骤

1. 听之前，考生应阅读题目说明，了解人物和背景信息，以联想对话情景。

2. 听第一遍录音，考生应听取对话大意，排除干扰项，选出每题的最佳选项。

3. 听第二遍录音，考生应注意听细节，核对已选择的答案是否正确。

注意事项

1. 题目中会有一个选项被当作例子，注意在选项中划掉，避免重复选择。

2. 卷面共有两列信息，每列的词汇都属于同一类别，如人物、物品、食物、事件等。

 样题解析

Questions 21 – 25

For each question, choose the correct answer.

You will hear Julia talking to her mother about a school fashion show.

What will each person help with?

Example:

0	Julia	D

People			Help with
21	Anton		A clothes
22	Emma		B food
			C lights
23	Karl		~~D make-up~~
24	Sarah		E music
			F photographs
25	George		G posters
			H tickets

解析

Step 1: 审题目，找关键

1. **背景信息** You will hear Julia talking to her mother about a school fashion show.

   • 关键信息：人物—Julia和her mother；事件—a school fashion show

   • 文本翻译：你会听到朱莉娅和她妈妈谈论学校的时装秀。

2. **题干** What will each person help with?

   • 关键信息：人物—each person；事件—help with

   • 文本翻译：每个人都会帮忙做什么？

3. 选项

- 左列：人物5个—Anton；Emma；Karl；Sarah；George
- 右列：事情8个—clothes（服装）；food（食物）；lights（灯光）；make up（化妆）；music（音乐）；photographs（摄影）；posters（海报）；tickets（票务）

Step 2：听录音，选答案

1. 听力原文

F1: We're having a fashion show at school again…

F2: Great. What are you helping with, Julia?

F1: I'm doing the make-up. I want it to be really good.

F2: That will be fun.

F1: [21]Anton wanted to have special lights but the teacher says we don't need them. So he's finding CDs to play in the show.

F2: Oh.

F1: [22]Emma chose really good music last year but she wants to take some pictures with her new camera this time.

F2: [23]Karl's a good photographer too, isn't he?

F1: [23]Yes, but he's drawing some posters. He's brilliant at art.

F2: [24]Is Sarah helping?

F1: [24]She's deciding what everyone will wear.

F2: Oh, will she be good at that? She was so good at selling tickets last time.

F1: Well, she's very interested in fashion now.

F2: Will there be a party afterwards?

F1: [25]George is going to get some snacks. It's difficult to know how many we'll need because we haven't sold many tickets yet.

F2: I'll buy one, how much are they...?

2. 选择答案

(21) Anton-E。对话中提到Anton时说"Anton wanted to have special lights but the teacher says we don't need them. So he's finding CDs to play in the show."。第一句中提到了"special lights"，但是注意后面用到了转折连词"but"，后面的信息是"老师说

我们不需要"，所以"lights"可排除。第二句中"so"后面的"finding CDs to play"，实际上表达的就是"music"，故选择E。

(22) Emma-F。对话中提到Emma时说"Emma chose really good music last year but she wants to take some pictures with her new camera this time."。同样，此处还是要重点关注"but"后面的信息，即"take some pictures"，可以对应到右列的"photographs"，故选F。

(23) Karl-G。对话中提到Karl时说"Karl's a good photographer too, isn't he?"。此处是一个问句，所以要关注该句的答句"Yes, but he's drawing some posters."。同样，"but"后面的为正确信息，即"Karl画海报"，正确答案为G。

(24) Sarah-A。对话中提到Sarah时说"She's deciding what everyone will wear."。注意本句中的"what everyone wear"指代的就是右列选项中的"clothes"，故选A。

(25) George-B。对话中提到George时说"George is going to get some snacks."。此处要理解核心词"snacks"的意思，即"零食"，属于food，故选择B。

Week 2 听力通关技巧

第2周目标

考试模块	时间	主题	内容	
Listening	Day 1	基础备考技巧	真题考点归纳、解题关键点	☐
	Day 2	学校主题技巧	真题相关话题、问题、词汇、短语等	☐
	Day 3	休闲主题技巧	真题相关话题、问题、词汇、短语等	☐
	Day 4	生活主题技巧	真题相关话题、问题、词汇、短语等	☐
	Day 5	社交主题技巧	真题相关话题、问题、词汇、短语等	☐
	Weekend	每周一练	基础热身训练	☐

Day 1　基础备考技巧

 考点汇总

　　剑桥A2 Key for Schools考试听力共涉及五大题型，在做每一类题目时，快速抓取题干信息或已给信息十分必要，现将真题中各个题型曾经出现过的问题类型以及问题考点归纳总结如下。

Part	问题类型	考点
Part 1 短对话图片单选题	What...?	物品、做的事情、吃的食物、买的东西、天气情况
	What time...?	比赛开始时间、见面时间
	Which...?	物品描述、运动类型、学校科目、电视节目、服装
	How...?	交通工具、做事方式
	How much...?	票价
	Where...?	物品位置、要去的地方、工作地点、所处位置
	Why...?	事情的原因

Part	问题类型	考点
Part 1 短对话图片单选题	When...?	派对时间
	Who...?	人物年龄、形象描述
Part 2 独白摘要题	... about	作业主题、测验主题、展览主题
	Dates	日期（月份、序数词）
	Time	时间（几点几分）、时长
	Name of...: Mr/Mrs...	人名
	Numbers	页码、人数、字数、电话号码
	Price	价格（折扣、单人价格、总价）
	Clothes	穿着要求
	Other information	目的地、网址、奖项、宾馆名称、天气、携带物品
Part 3 长对话单选题	疑问词提问	What/Where/Why/Which/How/When（穿着、地点、原因、活动、选择、方式、时间）
	陈述句缺失信息	补充时间、星期、年龄、位置、携带物品要求、同行人物、交通方式、食物饮品、观点态度
Part 4 短对话/独白单选题	疑问词提问（疑问词与Part 1类似）	购买/没买物品原因、出行目的地、讲话内容、要做的事情、情感表达、参加活动、工作职业
Part 5 信息匹配题	What sport / present / activity/opinion...?	人物与运动项目、人物与礼物、人物与活动、人物与观点态度
	What... bring...?	人物与携带物品
	Where...?	人物与地点

 ## 解题关键

答题通用步骤

审题 ➡ 听答 ➡ 检查

1. 审题。

✓ 审题目说明——了解人物、事件及场景等背景信息。

✓ 审题干——了解问题出题点及核心考查内容。

✓ 审选项——进一步熟悉即将听到的听力材料的内容，了解可能的正确答案是什么，在听录音时注意抓取。

2. 听答。

✓ 听录音，选择/填入正确答案。

3. 检查。

✓ 通常录音会播放两遍，在听第二遍录音时，边补充未答题目，边检查已作答题目。

以上三步完成后，最后将答案誊写到答题卡中。

答题信号词汇总

在听力考试中，几乎每道题都会出现连词、转折词等，通常这些单词后面紧跟的内容才是表达的重点或者正确答案，常用到的转折连词如下。

信号词	表达关系	含义	举例
but	表转折	但是，可是	We are leaving on Tuesday **but** we're returning on Friday instead of Thursday. 我们周二出发，但是我们是周五回来，而不是周四。
because, so	表因果	because 因为 so 所以	You should bring a swimsuit **because** if the weather's good, we'll dive off the boat. We have lots of towels, **so** there's no need to bring one. 你应该带上泳衣，因为如果天气好，我们就下船。我们有很多毛巾，所以没必要带毛巾了。
actually	表强调	实际上，其实	The phone was **actually** in the back of my dad's car. 手机其实在我爸爸的车后座。
instead (of)	表替代	代替；而不是	Mr Kennedy will be taking you **instead**. 肯尼迪先生将接管你们。
not... until/till	表强调	直到……才……	We **aren't** playing **till** half past three today. 我们今天直到三点半才开始比赛。

Day 2　学校主题技巧

 考场重现

听力考试中，"学校"是考试频次较高的一个主题，如学校的课程、课堂活动、课余活动、作业布置等都是经常考到的话题，现将曾考过的部分内容汇总如下。

Part	考查主题	问题举例
Part 1 短对话图片单选题	学科相关（如学科项目主题）	Which *subject* won't they study next year?
	课堂活动（如制作模型、观看影片等）	What did Helen's class *do in their history lesson*?
Part 2 独白摘要题	外出活动（如活动时间、着装要求、费用等）	You will hear a teacher talking to pupils about *a school trip.*
	家庭作业（如作业内容、要求等细节信息）	You will hear a teacher telling a class about some *homework.*
	学校测验（如测验主题、人数、奖项、人名等）	You will hear a student talking to her classmates about *a quiz.*
	图书馆（如营业时间、联系人人名等）	You will hear a teacher telling her class about *some changes to the school library.*
Part 3 长对话单选题	兴趣课程（如舞蹈课）	What does Michael *wear* to her dance classes?
	比赛（如写作比赛）	*How many words* do students have to write for the competition?
	旅行（如参观博物馆）	What does Lily *want to visit* on the next school trip?
Part 4 短对话/独白单选题	旅行及活动	Where are they going to go *on the school trip*?
	课程及作业	What should the girl *try to do in the future*?
	老师通知	What's he talking to them *about*?
Part 5 信息匹配题	学校活动准备（如旅行、学校表演、项目、运动会等）	You will hear two friends talking about *a school sports day.* What sport will each person do?

 ## 考点锦囊

关于"学校"主题常考的词汇或短语总结如下。

学校课程

course 课程；科	**subject** 科目；主题
lesson 课	**class** 班级
maths 数学	**physics** 物理学
chemistry 化学	**geography** 地理
biology 生物	**art** 美术
history 历史	**project** 项目

课堂活动及作业

---

enter a competition 参加比赛	exam 考试；检查
test 测试	teach 教
quiet 安静的	website 网址
watch a video 看视频	find out about 弄清楚关于……的情况
textbook 教科书	paragraph 段落
page 页码	discuss 讨论
interesting model 有趣的模型	get sth. right 把事情做好
make a poster 制作海报	school quiz 学校测验
leave a message 留言	understand 理解

 ## 热身演练

Complete the sentences with the words in the box. **用框中单词补全句子。**

| understand | message | discuss | interesting | quiet | website |

1. The book we are reading in class is really _____.

2. I couldn't _____ the meaning of the text, so I asked my teacher for help.

3. Could you please keep _____ during the class?

4. Can you give Jane a _____ for me? Tell her I've booked a tennis court for 8:00.

5. I'm very interested in your idea—shall we _____ it this afternoon?

6. I found this information on their _____.

Day 3 休闲主题技巧

 ## 考场重现

　　不管是听力的图片题还是对话选择题，又或是填空题、信息匹配题，常会出现涉及"运动、假期安排、周末活动、看电影、派对"等主题的听力素材，现将曾考过的部分内容汇总如下。

Part	考查主题	问题举例
Part 1 短对话图片单选题	假期活动（目的地、时间）	Where are the two friends going to go first today?
	运动项目	Which new sport is the girl going to do today?
	派对（时间、安排）	When is the party?
	电影电视（票价、节目）	Which programme will the two friends watch together?
Part 2 独白摘要题	出行准备	You will hear a girl called Sophia leaving a message for her friend.
Part 3 长对话单选题	假期俱乐部	Why didn't the girl go to the club last week?
	参观博物馆	What did Maria prefer at the museum?
	参加羽毛球比赛	How does Zac feel about the match?
Part 4 短对话/独白单选题	假期计划（周末活动、暑假安排、野餐准备）	What does the girl hope to do this summer?
	运动（游泳、网球比赛等）	How did he prepare for the match?
	电影（对电影看法）	What did the girl think about the film?
Part 5 信息匹配题	周末活动（活动类型、对参观地方的看法）	What was her opinion about her visit to each place?
	生日礼物	What present did she get from each person?

🎧 考点锦囊

关于"休闲娱乐"主题常考的词汇或短语总结如下。

活动场所

museum 博物馆	**castle** 城堡
farm 农场	**forest** 森林
valley 山谷	**cinema** 电影院
sports club 运动俱乐部	**beach** 海滩

娱乐项目

computer game 电脑游戏	**skateboarding** 滑板运动
ski 滑雪	**surf** 冲浪
surfboard 冲浪板	**play golf** 打高尔夫球

sailing 帆船运动	cycling 骑自行车
snowboarding 滑雪板运动	volleyball 排球
tennis court 网球场	space travel 太空旅行
play a board game 玩棋盘游戏	hockey 曲棍球

活动感受

tired 疲惫的	bored 厌烦的
worried 担心的	boring 令人厌烦的
funny 有趣的	crowded 拥挤的
exciting 令人兴奋的	scary 可怕的
noisy 嘈杂的	useful 有用的

🎧 热身演练

Read the descriptions and choose the correct words and phrases from the box. 阅读描述，从框中选择正确的单词。

valley	castle	crowded	surf	scary	ski

1. It's a large strong building built in the past by kings or queens. _____
2. It's a kind of water sports. _____
3. This is a sport related to snow. _____
4. It is used to describe something that makes me afraid. _____
5. having a lot of people _____
6. It's an area of low land between hills or mountains. _____

Day 4 　生活主题技巧

🎧 考场重现

考试中常会遇到有关"天气、购物、交通工具、选择礼物、饮食"等内容，现将曾考过的部分内容汇总如下。

Part	考查主题	问题举例
Part 1 短对话图片单选题	交通工具（上学、去音乐会）	How did the girl get to school this morning?
	购物（购买的物品、价格）	What does the boy's mother need to buy for him?
	饮食（早餐、午餐）	What did the boy eat for breakfast?
	放学回家（回家晚了、回家途中、到家后要做的事情）	Why did the girl come home late?
	天气情况	What was the weather like at the weekend?
Part 4 短对话/独白单选题	购物（选择礼物、购买理由）	Why did the girl choose the bag?
	饮食（在外用餐、在家烹饪）	What's the problem with their food?

 考点锦囊

关于"日常生活"主题常考的词汇或短语总结如下。

交通出行

train station 火车站	**take so long** 花费很长时间
taxi 出租车	**bus** 公交车
on one's way to... 去……的路上	**pick up sb.** 接上某人
give sb. a lift 让某人搭便车	**wait for** 等待
cycle path 自行车专用道	**catch the bus** 赶公交车
bus stop 公交车站	**by coach** 坐长途汽车

享用美食

lunch box 饭盒	**grape** 葡萄
cheese sandwich 奶酪三明治	**melon** 瓜
dessert 甜点	**breakfast/lunch/supper** 早餐/午餐/晚餐
flour 面粉	**pasta** 意大利面
vegetable 蔬菜	**a glass of juice** 一杯果汁
bake cake 烤蛋糕	**chocolate cake** 巧克力蛋糕
dried fruit 干果	**roast chicken** 烤鸡
sausage 香肠	**omelette** 煎蛋卷

	购物
look for 寻找	**present** 礼物
choose 选择	**right price** 合适的价格
right size 合适的尺寸	**sports kit** 运动套装
wrong colour 错误的颜色	**striped** 有条纹的

🎧 热身演练

Complete the sentences with the words or phrases in the box. **用框中单词或词组补全句子。**

vegetables	size	sports kit	lift	wait for	look for

1. I'm not sure where I left my phone. I need to _____ it before we leave.

2. Can you please give me a _____ to the airport tomorrow? My flight is early in the morning.

3. Don't forget to bring your _____ to the gym.

4. The _____ of the dress is too small, I need a larger one.

5. The supermarket has a wide variety of _____, from carrot to broccoli.

6. I'll be right here to _____ you. Take your time finishing your work.

Day 5　社交主题技巧

🎧 考场重现

听力考试中，尤其是涉及对话的听力素材，常会考到"人物描述、物品描述、工作职业、讨论兴趣爱好"等内容，现将曾考过的部分内容汇总如下。

Part	考查主题	问题举例
Part 1 短对话图片单选题	人物描述	Who is the girl going to meet?
	物品描述	Which photo is the boy showing his mother?
	会面安排（见面时间、地点）	What time will the friends meet tomorrow?

续表

Part	考查主题	问题举例
Part 4 短对话/独白单选题	讨论兴趣爱好（读书）	What does the boy say about the book he's just read?
	日常交流	What's the girl surprised about?
	工作职业	What job does Dan's mum do?

🎧 考点锦囊

关于"日常沟通及人际交往"主题常考的词汇或短语总结如下。

日常交流

be surprised about 对……感到惊讶	**incredible** 难以置信的
normally 通常地	**thereafter** 之后
run away 跑开了	**especially** 特别地
be full of 充满……	**suddenly** 突然地
be perfect for 非常适合……	**stand by** 站在……旁边
reception 接待	**hold on a moment** 稍等一下
as if 好像	**get off work** 下班
recently 最近	**hardly ever** 几乎没有
leave a message 留言	**wake up late** 起床晚了
look forward to 期待……	**slightly** 稍微
comfortable 舒服的	**remember / forget** 记住/忘记
as soon as 一……就……	**at least** 至少

处理问题

ask sb. a favour 请某人帮忙	**describe** 描述
explain clearly 清楚地解释	**save up** 储蓄
be absent from 缺席	**never mind** 不要紧
helpful 有帮助的	**walk down** 沿着……走
be/get ready to 准备好去做……	**problem** 问题
turn the volume down 把音量调低	**hurt** 受伤
realize 意识到	**unfortunately** 遗憾的是
run out 耗尽，用完	**engine** 发动机

热身演练

Complete the sentences with the phrases in the box. 用框中词组补全句子。

at least	save up	be absent from
turn the volume down	run out of	hold on a moment

1. When we want someone to wait for a short period of time in phone calls, we should say,

   "_____!"

2. Could you please _____? It's a bit too loud.

3. The meeting will last _____ until 9 p.m. So we'd better have dinner now.

4. I've _____ milk—would you like some creamer instead?

5. John _____ school yesterday because he was sick.

6. I want to buy a new car, so I should _____ money to do so.

Weekend 三

I. Complete the table with the words or phrases in the box. 用框中的单词或词组完成下列表格。

the museum	have a picnic	skateboarding	the castle
omelette	chocolate cake	dried fruit	go to a restaurant
have a party	a park	taking photos	surfing
the beach	sailing		

Hobbies	Places to go	Food	Things to do at the weekend

II. Match the questions (1–6) to the answers (a–f). 匹配问题与答案。

(   ) 1. How often do you have this chess lesson?

(   ) 2. Was it rainy in London last week, Linda?

(   ) 3. When do you have drawing lessons, John?

(   ) 4. What time does Jane's birthday party start on Saturday?

(   ) 5. How much did you pay for the computer game, Jason?

(   ) 6. What would you like for lunch?

---

a. The usual price is £30, but now it's half-price.

b. Once a week,and it's an eight-week course.

c. No, it wasn't. It was sunny.

d. Every Sunday. Do you want to come with me next week?

e. At about 18:00, but I'm meeting Nancy at the station at 15:30 and we're going together.

f. Can I have some of those sausages in the fridge?

III. Listen and choose the correct picture. 听录音选择正确的图片。

1.
A   B   C

2.
A   B   C

3.
A   B   C

4. What will the weather be like tomorrow?

A   B   C

5. How does the boy usually go home?

A    B    C

IV. Listen and choose the correct answer. 听录音选择正确的答案。

1. When did Peter visit his grandparents?

   A. Last Sunday afternoon.

   B. Last Saturday.

   C. Last Sunday morning.

2. Why did the boy look tired?

   A. Because he stayed up.

   B. Because he had a bad cold.

   C. Because he didn't have enough sleep.

3. What happened to the woman?

   A. She forgot to put her wallet in her bag.

   B. She couldn't find her wallet.

   C. She didn't know where to put her wallet.

4. When will Ms. Zhang fly to New York?

   A. On October 3rd.

   B. On October 30th.

   C. On October 13rd.

5. How much should the man pay?

   A. $ 5.

   B. $ 9.

   C. $ 4.5.

短对话图片单选题

第3周目标

考试模块	时间	主题	内容	
Part 1 短对话图片 选择题	Day 1	休闲娱乐	What's Julia going to do tonight?	☐
	Day 2	时间安排	What time does the art lesson start?	☐
	Day 3	健康运动	What will Chloe do on Saturday?	☐
	Day 4	购物买单	How much are the shorts?	☐
	Day 5	人物描述	Who will meet Peter at the airport?	☐
	Weekend	每周一练	基础训练及模拟训练	☐

Day 1　休闲娱乐

 考场模拟

For each question, choose the correct picture.

What's Julia going to do tonight?

A　　　　　　　　　　B　　　　　　　　　　C

🎧 思路点拨

Step 1:【审题目，找关键】

1. **题干** What's Julia going to do tonight?

   - 关键信息：人物—Julia；时间—tonight

   - 题干翻译：今天晚上Julia准备做什么？

2. **选项**

   - 图片A：卧病在床—ill

   - 图片B：参加聚会—go to the party

   - 图片C：看书学习—study or do homework

Step 2:【听录音，选答案】

1. **听力原文**

   M: Are you going to go to the party tonight, Julia?

   F: <u>I'd love to, but I can't. I couldn't go to school when I was ill last week, so I have a lot of</u>

   <u>homework to do.</u>

   M: But you are feeling better?

   F: Much better, but I still feel tired.

2. **选择答案**

   - 首先出现选项B，go to the party，但是Julia回答："I'd love to, but I can't."。由此可排除选项B。

   - 其次出现选项A，I couldn't go to school when I was ill last week. 根据关键信息"was ill"和"last week"可判断生病是上周的事情，和题干的关键信息"tonight"不相符，故排除选项A。

   - 接下来出现选项C，so I have a lot of home work to do. 由此得知，Julia上周因为生病没去学校，有很多作业要做。所以今天晚上Julia要做作业，正确答案为C。

【Answer key】C

百变演练

I. Match the words or phrases with the pictures. 将单词或短语与相应的图片连线。

do homework	go to the party	ill

II. Listen and choose the right picture. 听录音选择正确的图片。

1. □   □

2. □   □

 考点锦囊

　　休闲娱乐场景涉及的活动很多，如参加各种各样的俱乐部课程、观看节目展览、举办和参加生日派对、开展个人兴趣爱好等。

活动	
go fishing 去钓鱼	**music club** 音乐俱乐部
after school 放学后	**listen to music** 听音乐
spare time 业余时间	**big football fan** 狂热的足球迷
cross the river 过河	**find out about** 了解
go to the party 参加派对	**get bored** 觉得无聊

Day 2 时间安排

 考场模拟

For each question, choose the correct picture.

What time does the art lesson start?

A   B   C

 思路点拨

Step 1:【审题目，找关键】

1. **题干** What **time** does the **art lesson start**?

   - 关键信息：问题—time；事项—art lesson；动作—start

   - 题干翻译：美术课什么时候开始？

2. **选项**

   - 图片A：两点半—half past two

   - 图片B：三点整—three

   - 图片C：三点半—half past three

Step 2:【听录音，选答案】

1. **听力原文**

   M: What time is it, Maria?

   F: It's half past two. Why?

   M: I want to go to that extra art lesson this afternoon. It starts at three, doesn't it?

   F: It's starting now and you're late! Be quick because it finishes at half past three.

2. 选择答案

- 首先出现选项A，half past two，双方谈论的是说话时的时间。

- 其次出现选项B，It starts at three, doesn't it? 此处虽然出现了题干中的关键词 "start" 以及选项中的时间 "three"，但是结尾处用的是反义疑问句 "doesn't it"，其目的是确定是否为三点钟开始。根据下面的回答 "It's starting now and you're late!" 可知，并不是三点开始，而是两人对话时已经开始。故排除选项B。而两人对话的时间在刚开始时已经提到，即 "half past two"，所以正确答案为A。

- 最后出现选项C，half past three。对话最后提到，"Be quick because it finishes at half past three."。注意句中的关键词 "finishes"，和 "start" 相对应，表示结束的时间。故排除选项C。

【 Answer key 】A

 百变演练

I. Look at the picture and write the correct phrase. 看图写出正确的词组。

1. _____

2. _____

II. Listen and choose the correct picture. 听录音选择正确的图片。

1.   ☐   ☐

2.　　　　　　□　　　　　　　　　　　□

 考点锦囊

1. **图片选择题中经常会考到选择钟表上时间的题目。在表达时间时，我们常用到的单词如下。**

o'clock（……点钟）　　half（……点半）　　quarter（一刻钟/十五分钟）

past（过……分钟）　　to（还差……分钟）

hour（小时）　　minute（分钟）　　second（秒钟）

2. **在听力原文中，具体的读法有以下几种方式。**

读法	适用场景	举例
【小时+分钟】直接读	所有	7:20→seven twenty 6:30→six thirty
【分钟＋past＋小时】	所表述的时间在半小时之内	7:20→twenty past seven 9:10→ten past nine
【half＋past＋小时】	所表述的时间恰好为半小时	6:30→half past six 10:30→half past ten
【（相差的）分钟＋to＋（下一）小时】	所表述的时间在半小时之外	8:40→twenty to nine 5:35→twenty-five to six
【小时（＋o'clock）】	时间为整点	2:00→two (o'clock)

Day 3　健康运动

 考场模拟

For each question, choose the correct picture.

　　What will Chloe do on Saturday?

A   B   C

 思路点拨

Step 1:【审题目，找关键】

1. **题干：** What will **Chloe** do **on Saturday**?

   - 关键信息：人物—Chloe；时间—on Saturday

   - 题干翻译：克洛伊周六将要做什么？

2. **选项：**

   - 图片A：玩滑板—skateboard

   - 图片B：骑自行车—ride a bike

   - 图片C：打篮球—play basketball

Step 2:【听录音，选答案】

1. **听力原文：**

   F: I've just been to the new skate park. It's great!

   M: Really, Chloe. I'm going there on Saturday. I'm going to go by bike. Do you want to come, too?

   F: I'd really like to but I'm playing in the school basketball team on that day. Why don't you ask Pete? He's got a new skateboard.

   M: Okay, I will.

2. **选择答案：**

   - 首先出现选项B，I'm going to go by bike. 根据说话者说的"Really, Chloe."可知说话者并不是Chloe，故排除选项B。

   - 其次出现选项C，I'd really like to but I'm playing in the school basketball team on that day. 注意这句话中的关键转折词"but"，引出了Chloe要参加的活动是"打篮球"，

句中的 "on that day" 指代的是上一个人说的 "on Saturday"。故选项C为正确答案。

● 最后出现选项A，He's got a new skateboard. 注意本句的主语是he，指的是上一句中提到的 "Pete"。故排除选项A。

【Answer key】C

 百变演练

I. Match the words or phrases with the pictures. 将单词或短语与相应的图片连线。

| ride a bike | go skateboarding | play basketball |

II. Listen and fill in the blanks. 听录音填空。

1. He sometimes goes _____ on weekends.

2. Why don't we _____ _____ this afternoon?

 考点锦囊

听力中遇到运动相关的情景时，常会考查运动的类型如下。

运动	
go skateboarding 滑滑板	**climb** 攀登
go swimming 去游泳	**play tennis** 打网球
play football 踢足球	**play basketball** 打篮球
play golf 打高尔夫球	**horse-riding** 骑马
box 拳击	**play baseball** 打棒球
bicycle 骑自行车	**play badminton** 打羽毛球
play volleyball 打排球	**sailing** 帆船运动

Day 4 购物买单

 考场模拟

For each question, choose the correct picture.

How much are the shorts?

£5	**£15**	**£20**
A	B	C

 思路点拨

Step 1:【审题目，找关键】

1. **题干：** **How much** are the **shorts**?

   - 关键信息：物品—shorts；问题—how much

   - 题干翻译：短裤多少钱?

2. **选项：**

   - 图片A：5英镑—five pounds

   - 图片B：15英镑—fifteen pounds

   - 图片C：20英镑—twenty pounds

Step 2:【听录音，选答案】

1. **听力原文：**

   M: Excuse me, are these shorts in the sale?

   F: Yes, sir. Everything on that shelf is five pounds.

   M: I'll take this shirt, too.

   F: That's fifteen pounds, so with the shorts that will be twenty pounds.

   M: Great, I'll take them.

2. 选择答案：

- 首先出现选项A，Everything on that shelf is five pounds. 根据上一句男士的问题"Are these shorts in the sale?"可知，男士询问的是"shorts（短裤）"，所以女士回复的"架子上的货品都是5英镑"指的就是"shorts"的价格，故选项A为正确答案。

- 其次出现选项B，That's fifteen pounds. 男士上一句提到还要购买"shirt（衬衣）"，女士回复"衬衣的价格是15英镑"，所以排除选项B。

- 最后出现选项C，so with the shorts that will be twenty pounds. 注意此处再次出现了题干中的"shorts"，但此处表达的是"加上衬衣一共是20英镑"，衬衣是15英镑，由此可再次确定短裤是5英镑，故排除选项C。

【Answer key】A

 百变演练

I. Translate. 翻译。

1. These shorts are in the sale.

_____

2. I'll take the shirt and the shorts.

_____

II. Listen and choose the correct answer. 听录音选择正确的答案。

1. How much does the shirt cost?

　　A. Fifteen pounds.　　　　B. Five pounds.　　　　C. Twenty pounds.

2. Which one is correct?

　　A. The man spent fifteen pounds on shorts.

　　B. The shirt and the shorts are both on sale.

　　C. The man finally paid twenty pounds.

考点锦囊

当图片显示为价格时，可提前预测以下相关信息。

1. 涉及场景：购票价格、用餐消费、购物结账、活动费用等。

2. 购物买单关键词：

How much...? ……多少钱？	cost 花费	price 价格
too much 太多了（通常表示价格太贵）	on sale 特价	take 购买
bill 账单	ticket 票	for sale 出售
change 零钱	expensive 昂贵的	cheap 便宜的
cash 现金	penny 便士	cent 分，美分

3. 注意区分以下三种货币符号：

dollar 美元（＄）   pound 英镑（£）   euro 欧元（€）

4. 注意听价格数字，包括整数和小数部分，以及它们之间的分隔符（例如逗号、点号等）。

整数：直接读，如"£5"就是five pounds。

带有小数点：两种读法，如"£7.50"可读作seven pounds fifty或seven fifty。

5. 注意听折扣信息，如学生身份可以享受的折扣、店里打折促销等；注意关键词 student（学生）、percent（百分比）、reduction（削减，减价）、discount（折扣）等。

Day 5 人物描述

 考场模拟

For each question, choose the correct picture.

Who will meet Peter at the airport?

A   B   C

思路点拨

Step 1:【审题目，找关键】

1. **题干：** Who will **meet Peter** at the **airport**?

- 关键信息：人物—Peter；地点—airport；事件—meet Peter
- 题干翻译：谁将在机场接彼得？

2. **选项：**

- 图片A：一个女人
- 图片B：一个男人
- 图片C：一男一女

Step 2:【听录音，选答案】

1. **听力原文：**

F: Will someone meet you when you arrive at the airport, Peter?

M: Yes. My parents will be at work, but my older sister will. She's just passed her driving test!

F: That's good news.

M: And my grandfather lives near the airport so we're going to visit him on the way home.

F: That's nice.

2. **选择答案：**

- 首先出现选项C，my parents。对话一开始，女士问男士，"Peter，你到机场的时候有人接你吗？"由此可知，对话中的男士就是Peter，即题干中提到要被接的人。Peter回答说"My parents will be at work, but my older sister will."。由此可知，Peter的父母要工作没有时间，故排除选项C。
- 其次出现选项A，my older sister。Peter的回答中提到"but my older sister will"，由此可知，Peter的姐姐会去接他。故选项A为正确答案。
- 最后出现选项B，my grandfather。Peter后面又提到"my grandfather lives near the airport"。注意此句中虽然出现了题干的关键信息"airport"，但只是说自己的爷爷住在机场附近，Peter和姐姐会在回家的路上去拜访他。因此可以排除选项B。

【Answer key】A

🎧 百变演练

I. Translate. 翻译。

1. My older sister will meet me when I arrive at the airport.

_____

2. My parents will be at work that day.

_____

3. We plan to visit our grandparents on the way home.

_____

II. Listen and tick or cross. 听录音判断正误。

1. Peter's parents has just passed her driving test.　　　　(　)

2. Peter's parents and his sister will meet him at the airport.　　(　)

3. Peter's grandfather lives near the airport.　　　　(　)

🎧 考点锦囊

当图片显示为人物时，通常会涉及对人物形象的描述以及人物关系的描述。

人物形象	
short 矮的，短的	**slim** 苗条的
tall 高的	**thin** 瘦的
beard 胡须	**long** 长的
blonde hair 金发	**short dark hair** 深色短发
short hair 短发	**long black hair** 黑色长发

人物关系	
family members 家庭成员	**parents** 父母
brother 兄弟	**sister** 姐妹
grandfather/grandad/grandpa（外）祖父	**grandmother/grandma**（外）祖母
cousin 堂兄弟姐妹	**grandchild** 孙子（女）；外孙（女）

Weekend 三

I. Match the questions(1-8) to the answers(a-h). 匹配问题与答案。

(　　) 1. How did they get home from the cinema?

(　　) 2. Where did the man find his phone?

(　　) 3. What will the girl do after school?

(　　) 4. What did the girl eat for lunch?

(　　) 5. What was the weather like at the weekend?

(　　) 6. How much were Jim's sports shoes?

(　　) 7. When is the boy going to the dentist?

(　　) 8. What's the matter with the girl?

a. On the sofa.	b. By taxi.
c. It was windy and cold.	d. They cost $80.
e. She ate a piece of pizza.	f. She has a headache.
g. On October 10th.	h. Finish her homework first and then watch TV.

II. Read the descriptions and choose the correct words from the box. 阅读描述，从框中选择正确的单词。

storm	cinema	customer	cash	guitar	library

1. It's a building in which films are shown. _____

2. People learn to play music on this. _____

3. You pay with this, not cheques or credit cards. _____

4. If you like reading books, you might go to this building. _____

5. This person buys things in a shop. _____

6. It's a very bad weather with strong winds and rain. _____

III. Look at the picture and complete the sentences. 看图补全句子。

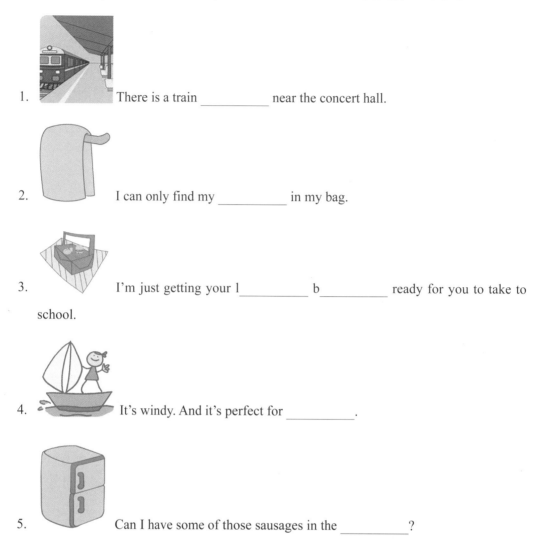

1. There is a train _____ near the concert hall.

2. I can only find my _____ in my bag.

3. I'm just getting your l_____ b_____ ready for you to take to school.

4. It's windy. And it's perfect for _____.

5. Can I have some of those sausages in the _____?

IV. Listen and choose the correct picture for each question. 听录音，并针对每个问题选择正确的图片。

1. How does the girl go to school now?

A   B   C

2. What time did the first class begin?

A

B

C

3. Where did Linda stay yesterday?

A

B

C

4. What can Bob do every day at home?

A

B

C

5. What will the weather be like next Sunday?

A

B

C

独白摘要题

第4周目标				
考试模块	时间	主题	内容	
	Day 1	假期活动	Jobs for students with Sunshine Holidays	☐
	Day 2	假期活动	考点锦囊及百变演练	☐
	Day 3	比赛通知	Short-film-making Competition	☐
Part 2 独白摘要 填空题	Day 4	比赛通知	考点锦囊及百变演练	☐
	Day 5	学校课程	Guitar Lessons	☐
	Day 6	学校课程	考点锦囊及百变演练	☐
	Weekend	每周一练	基础训练及模拟训练	☐

Day 1 假期活动 · 考场模拟

 考场模拟

Questions 6 – 10

For each question, write the correct answer in the gap. Write **one word** or a **number** or a **date** or a **time**.

You will hear a teacher talking to a group of students about summer jobs.

Jobs for students with Sunshine Holidays	
Work in:	Children's summer camps
Dates of jobs:	(6) 15th June-20th _____
Staff must be:	(7) _____ years old

Staff must be able to:	(8) _____
Staff will earn:	(9) £ _____ per week
Send a letter and:	(10) _____

🎧 思路点拨

Step 1:【审题目，找关键】

1. **文本：** You will hear a teacher talking to a group of students about summer jobs.

   - 关键信息：主题—summer jobs（暑期工作）。
   - 题干翻译：你会听到一位老师在和一群学生谈论暑期工作。

2. **图表：**

   (6) Dates of jobs—工作日期，15th June-20th—6月15日到_____20日；结合两点，此处要填入"**月份**"。

   (7) Staff must be—员工必须是，years old—_____岁；此空要填入"**年龄数字**"。

   (8) Staff must be able to—员工必须能够；此空要填入"**能够做的事情（对员工的能力要求）**"。

   (9) Staff will earn—员工会赚取，£_____per week—每周_____英镑；此空要填入"**金钱数字**"。

   (10) Send a letter and—发送一封信和_____；此空要填入和letter并列的"**物品**"。

Step 2:【听录音，选答案】

1. **听力原文：**

   F: Several students from this college went to work for Sunshine Holidays last year and enjoyed it. So I'm going to give you some information about working in their summer camps this year.

   (6) The camps start on the fifteenth of June so you must be free from then until August the twentieth. Most students then spend September travelling around and having a holiday before they come home.

   (7) The camps are for children who are between ten and fifteen years old and to work there you have to be nineteen. So that's OK for most of you.

   You don't need to be good at sports or languages (8) but they only want people who can drive. That's because you'll take the children out on trips by car.

(9) Each week you'll get sixty-five pounds, so you could save over five hundred pounds during your time there.

If you're interested, (10) you need to write a letter and send it with a photo to Sunshine Holidays. So, does anyone have any questions…?

2. **填入答案：**

(6) 录音中提到，露营于6月15日开始，该信息与空格前的"15th June"相符。后面提到"so you must be free from then until August the twentieth"，该句中"then"指代前面的"15th June"，"until"后面是空格处需填入的信息，即"August the twentieth"，故应填入AUGUST。

(7) 此空是询问"员工"的年龄，录音中提到两处年龄，第一处"ten and fifteen years old"指参加露营的孩子的年龄，第二处才是"员工"的年龄，注意"to work there"就指的是"staff"，根据"you have to be nineteen"可知，此空应填入19或NINETEEN。

(8) 此空是询问对员工的能力要求。录音中虽先提到了"be good at sports or languages"，但是前面是否定"don't need to"，可排除。紧接着是转折连词"but"，需注意后面的信息，"they only want people who can drive"，此处的"can"与表中的"be able to"相同，故应填入DRIVE。

(9) 录音中在提到薪资时说，"Each week you'll get sixty-five pounds."。本句中的"each week"与题目中的"per week"意思相同，故应填入65或SIXTY-FIVE。

(10) 录音最后提到"you need to write a letter and send it with a photo"，所以空格处和"letter"并列的物品应该是"photo"，故应填入PHOTO或PHOTOGRAPH。

【 Answer key 】

(6) AUGUST   (7) 19 / NINETEEN   (8) DRIVE

(9) 65 / SIXTY-FIVE   (10) PHOTO / PHOTOGRAPH

假期活动 · 考点锦囊

 考点锦囊

摘要填空中经常会考到月、日、星期等相关内容。

1. Day和Date的区别。

Date—具体日期，即"几月几日"，如August 20th（8月20日）。

Day—星期，如Monday（星期一）。

2. 关于月份和星期的相关单词如下。

Month 月份	January 一月	February 二月	March 三月
	April 四月	May 五月	June 六月
	July 七月	August 八月	September 九月
	October 十月	November 十一月	December 十二月
Week 星期	Monday 星期一	Tuesday 星期二	Wednesday 星期三
	Thursday 星期四	Friday 星期五	Saturday 星期六
	Sunday 星期日		

3. 在录音中，日期通常有两种读法。

读法规则	举例	读法
月 + the + 日	6月15日	June the fifteenth
the + 日 + of + 月	8月20日	the twentieth of August

4. 真题中考查时间相关内容时，小标题内容如下。

标题	说明
Date first course starts	第一门课程开始的日期（月份和天）
On Tuesdays, library closes at	星期二，图书馆闭馆的时间（具体几点几分）
Time to arrive at school by	到达学校的时间（具体几点几分）
Length of tour	旅游时长（具体多少分钟）
Time to be at school	该去上学的时间（具体几点几分）

百变演练

I. Match the words in the box to the descriptions. 根据下面的描述匹配框中的单词。

| several | August | drive | hundred | photograph |

1. the 8th month of the year _____

2. a photo _____

3. 100 _____

4. more than two but not very many _____

5. to operate a car _____

II. Listen and complete the sentence. 听录音补全句子。

1. The camps _____ on the fifteenth of June.

2. Most students then spend _____ travelling around and having a holiday before they come home.

3. You must be good at _____ or languages.

4. You could save over _____ _____ pounds during your time there.

5. Several students from this college went to work for Sunshine Holidays last year and _____ it.

III. Listen and write T or F. 听录音判断正误。

(   ) 1. The camps start on June 15th and end on August 20th.

(   ) 2. The camps are for children between five and ten years old.

(   ) 3. Students need to be at least 19 years old to work in the camps.

(   ) 4. The camps require employees to be good at sports and languages.

(   ) 5. The pay for a week of work in the camps is £65.

Day 3 | 比赛通知 · 考场模拟

 考场模拟

Questions 6 – 10

For each question, write the correct answer in the gap. Write **one word** or a **number** or a **date** or a **time**.

You will hear a teacher telling some boys and girls about a short-film-making competition.

SHORT-FILM-MAKING COMPETITION	
Last year's films about:	plants
This year's films about:	(6) _____
Send films to:	(7) school _____
Competition on August's last:	(8) _____
Number of prizes:	(9) _____
First prize:	(10) _____

 思路点拨

Step 1:【审题目，找关键】

1. **文本：** You will hear a teacher telling some boys and girls about a short-film-making competition.

   • 关键信息：主题—short-film-making competition（短片制作比赛）

   • 题干翻译：你会听到一位老师向一些男孩和女孩讲述一场短片制作比赛。

2. **图表：**

   (6) This year's films about—今年影片是关于_____；此处要填入"**短片主题**"。

   (7) Send films to—将影片发送到_____；此空要填入"**影片接收者**"。

   (8) Competition on August's last—比赛在八月的最后一个_____；此空要填入"**比**

赛举办的时间"。

(9) Number of prizes——奖项数量是＿＿＿＿＿＿；此空要填入"**数字**"。

(10) First prize——一等奖是＿＿＿＿＿＿；此空要填入"**奖品**"。

Step 2:【听录音，选答案】

1. 听力原文：

F: Hello everybody. I'm going to give you some information about this year's short-film-making competition. As you may remember, know, last year's films are about plants; (6) but this year, students have to make a short film focused on animals. You can choose to make a film of cats or dogs and (7) send it to the school office from August 15th to August 20th. (8) The competition will be on the last Wednesday of August.

The students who want to take part in the competition must send two short films, but only one will be chosen for the competition. The winners will receive an email message before the competition day. (9) There will be three prizes: the third prize is a T-shirt; the second prize is a cup and (10) the winner of this year's competition will get a backpack.

Lastly, remember to tell your family and friends that the short film exhibition will be held on the third floor of the school. Now, if you have any questions, I'll be happy to answer all of them.

2. 填入答案：

(6) 录音中提到，去年影片主题为"植物"，后面用到转折连词"but"，注意后面的信息"this year, students have to make a short film focused on animals"，该句中"focused on"与"about"意思相近，都有"关于"的含义，故应填入ANIMALS。

(7) 录音在描述完影片主题的要求后，提到"send it to the school office"，由此得知，要将影片发送到学校办公室，空格前有"school"，故空格处应填入OFFICE。

(8) 此空是询问比赛的时间。录音中虽先提到了"August 15th"和"August 20th"这两个时间，但这个时间区间是提交影片作品的时间。后面提到"The competition will be on the last Wednesday of August."，结合题干，此处应填入WEDNESDAY。

(9) 录音中在提到比赛奖项时说"There will be three prizes."。由此得知，比赛奖项的数量为3个，故应填入3或THREE。

(10) 录音中在介绍具体三个奖项的内容时提到"the winner of this year's competition will

get a backpack"，"the winner of the competition" 指的就是"first prize"，故空格处应填入BACKPACK。

【Answer key】

(6) ANIMALS　　(7) OFFICE　　(8) WEDNESDAY　　(9) 3 / THREE　　(10) BACKPACK

Day 4　比赛通知·考点锦囊

 考点锦囊

在听力中遇到与比赛相关的通知信息时，常会涉及比赛类型、参加比赛的详细要求（时间、地点、资格）以及比赛的奖项设置等信息。

比赛类型	
a basketball match 篮球比赛	a short story competition 短故事比赛
a boat race 划船比赛	a football match 足球比赛
a swimming competition/race 游泳比赛	a surfing competition 冲浪比赛
a cycle race 自行车比赛	a writing competition 写作比赛
a singing competition 唱歌比赛	a cooking competition 烹饪比赛
a painting competition 绘画比赛	a sports competition 体育比赛
a dancing competition 舞蹈比赛	a music competition 音乐比赛

参加比赛	
team 团队	take part in 参加
come first/second/third in a competition 在比赛中获得第一名/第二名/第三名	enter a competition 参加比赛
stadium 体育场	player 运动员
against 和……比赛	run a race 参加赛跑

比赛结果

win a competition 赢得比赛   win the race 赢得比赛

lose the race 输掉比赛   winner 获胜者

result 结果   prize 奖品

medal 奖牌   first prize 一等奖

the top prize 一等奖，最高奖   win second prize 获得二等奖

🎧 百变演练

I. Match the words in the box to the descriptions. 根据下面的描述匹配框中的单词。

| choose | exhibition | remember | Wednesday | Thursday |

1. the day after Tuesday   _____

2. to not forget   _____

3. pick out sth.   _____

4. a collection of things for public display   _____

5. the fifth day of the week   _____

II. Listen and complete the sentence. 听录音补全句子。

1. I'm going to give you some information about this year's short-film-making _____.

2. The students who want to _____ _____ _____ the competition must send two short films.

3. The winners will receive an email _____ before the competition day.

4. The _____ of this year's competition will get a backpack.

5. The short film exhibition will be _____ on the third floor of the school.

III. Listen and write T or F. 听录音判断正误。

(   ) 1. Last year's short film competition was about plants.

(   ) 2. This year, students can choose to make a film about either cats or dogs.

(   ) 3. The deadline to submit films to the school office is August 15th.

(   ) 4. Each student can only send one short film for the competition.

(   ) 5. The winner of this year's competition will receive a T-shirt.

 Day 5 学校课程 · 考场模拟

考场模拟

Questions 6 – 10

For each question, write the correct answer in the gap. Write **one word** or a **number** or a **date** or a **time**.

You will hear a teacher telling his students about guitar lessons.

GUITAR LESSONS	
Teacher's name:	Mrs Halliday
Day:	(6) _____
Price per hour:	(7) £ _____
Place of lesson:	(8) _____ Main Street
Teacher's phone number:	(9) _____
Must call between:	(10) _____ and nine

思路点拨

Step 1:【审题目，找关键】

1. **文本：** You will hear a teacher telling his students about guitar lessons.

   - 关键信息：主题—guitar lessons（吉他课）
   - 题干翻译：你会听到一位老师向他的学生讲述吉他课。

2. **图表：**

   (6) Day—天；此处要填入"**星期几**"。(如果是Date，则需要填写具体的日期)

   (7) Price per hour—每小时的价格；此空要填入"**价格数字**"。

   (8) Place of lesson—上课的地点；此空要填入"**地点**"。

(9) Teacher's phone number—老师的电话号码；此空要填入"**电话号码数字**"。

(10) Must call between—必须在_____打电话；结合空格后面的and nine可知，此空要填入"**时间数字**"。

Step 2:【听录音，选答案】

1. 听力原文：

F: Good morning, boys and girls. As you know, you all have the possibility to join Mrs Halliday's guitar lessons, starting from next month. That's H-A-double L-I-D-A-Y.

Lessons are on Wednesdays and Fridays, but on Wednesdays you already have the Spanish course with Mr Sheldon, (6) so your day will definitely be Friday.

Now, the price. (7) A single lesson for three students is 35 pounds an hour or £20 for half an hour. I suggest you start with the one-hour lesson, then once you know the basics you can do half an hour.

You must go to Mrs Halliday's house which is very close to Queen Shopping Mall. (8) The exact address is 205 Main Street. If you're interested in learning to play guitar, please give her a call. (9) Her number is 0865 945371. Did you get it right? I'll say it again: 0865 945371. (10) The best time to call her is between seven and nine. Is that clear to everyone?

2. 填入答案：

(6) 录音中提到了"Wednesday"和"Friday"两个时间，接着用到了转折连词"but"，后面的信息说明"Wednesday"有西班牙语的课程，所以"your day will definitely be Friday"，单词"definitely"表示"当然地，一定地"，故此空应填入FRIDAY。

(7) 根据题干信息可知，此空是询问一小时课程的价格，录音中提到"35 pounds an hour"和"20 pounds for half an hour"。此处"an hour"就等同于题干中的"per hour"，故应填入35或THIRTY-FIVE。

(8) 此空是询问上课的地址。录音中提到了"The exact address is 205 Main Street."，题干中的"place"和句中的"exact address"表达同一含义，结合空格后面的"Main Street"，可知此处应填入205。

(9) 录音中在提到电话号码相关的信息时说"give her a call(给她打电话)"，考生听到该信息时，就要注意记录。接着说出了电话号码"Her number is 0865 945371."，后面又对该号码再次重复了一遍。故正确答案是<u>0865 945371</u>。

(10) 录音在说完老师的电话号码后，又提到"The best time to call her is between seven and nine."。所以给老师致电的最佳时间段是"between seven and nine"，故应填入<u>7 / SEVEN</u>。

【Answer key】

| (6) FRIDAY | (7) 35 / THIRTY-FIVE | (8) 205 | (9) 0865 945371 | (10) 7 / SEVEN |

Day 6　学校课程·考点锦囊

考点锦囊

除了日期和星期等，摘要题中还经常会考查数字相关的信息，如电话号码、房间号、年龄、人数、字数、页数等，问题多伴随number出现。

1. 电话号码：

➤ 电话号码的数字通常比较多，常会出现相邻重复的数字，这时录音中会用double表示，在答题时需注意双写数字，比如double eight就要写成"88"。

➤ 数字"0"在录音中有两种读法：字母O或者zero。

➤ 录音中读长串的电话号码时，通常是三位或者四位一读，比如0885945371读作zero-double eight-five，nine-four-five，three-seven-one。

2. 其他数字：

数词书写时，既可写阿拉伯数字（如20），也可写英文（如TWENTY）。

注意区分-teen"十几"和-ty"几十"的发音区别。

thirteen (13) [ˌθɜːˈtiːn]	thirty (30) [ˈθɜːti]
fourteen (14) [ˌfɔːˈtiːn]	forty (40) [ˈfɔːti]
fifteen (15) [ˌfɪfˈtiːn]	fifty (50) [ˈfɪfti]
sixteen (16) [ˌsɪksˈtiːn]	sixty (60) [ˈsɪksti]
seventeen (17) [ˌsevnˈtiːn]	seventy (70) [ˈsevnti]
eighteen (18) [ˌeɪˈtiːn]	eighty (80) [ˈeɪti]
nineteen (19) [ˌnaɪnˈtiːn]	ninety (90) [ˈnaɪnti]

3. 基数词和序数词汇总

基数词			序数词		
1～10	11～19	20～100	第1～第10	第11～第19	第20～第100
one	eleven		first	eleven**th**	
two	twelve	twen**ty**	second	twelf**th**	twentie**th**
three	thir**teen**	thir**ty**	third	thirteen**th**	thirtie**th**
four	four**teen**	for**ty**	fourth	fourteen**th**	fortie**th**
five	fif**teen**	fif**ty**	fifth	fifteen**th**	fiftie**th**
six	six**teen**	six**ty**	sixth	sixteen**th**	sixtie**th**
~~seven~~	seven**teen**	seven**ty**	seventh	seventeen**th**	seventie**th**
eight	eigh**teen**	eigh**ty**	eighth	eighteen**th**	eightie**th**
nine	nine**teen**	nine**ty**	ninth	nineteen**th**	ninetie**th**
ten		hundred			hundred**th**

🎧 百变演练

I. Match the words in the box to the descriptions. 根据下面的描述匹配框中的单词。

> mall   suggest   possibility   definitely   course

1. a series of lessons _____

2. a large shopping centre _____

3. without question _____

4. to advise _____

5. a thing that may happen _____

II. Listen and complete the sentence. 听录音补全句子。

1. As you _____, you all have the possibility to _____ Mrs Halliday's guitar lessons.

2. Lessons are on _____ and _____.

3. A single lesson for three students is £20 for _____ _____ _____.

4. You must go to Mrs Halliday's house which is very _____ _____ Queen Shopping Mall.

5. If you're _____ in learning to play guitar, please give her a call.

III. Listen and write T or F. 听录音判断正误。

(   ) 1. Mrs Halliday's guitar lessons start next week.

(   ) 2. The Spanish course is on Wednesdays.

(   ) 3. The price for a one-hour lesson is £35.

(   ) 4. Mrs Halliday's house is far from Queen Shopping Mall.

(   ) 5. The best time to call Mrs Halliday is at six o'clock.

Weekend 二

I. Complete the table with the words and phrases in the box. 用方框中的单词和短语完成表格。

last year	Monday morning	half past nine	February
the afternoon	20th August	2024	Fridays
yesterday	the moment		

at	in	on	无介词

II. Complete the sentences with the numbers, months or days. 用数字、月份以及星期补全句子。

1. Jenny is ten years old. And she will have her _____ birthday party next week.

2. When it's 10:45, it is also a quarter to _____.

3. There are _____ minutes in an hour.

4. There are _____ months in a year.

5. The listening paper is the _____ part of the KET exam.

6. *D* is the _____ letter of the alphabet.

7. Teachers' Day is on the tenth of _____.

8. There are _____ letters in the alphabet.

9. The eleventh month of the year is _____.

10. The day of the week before Thursday and following Tuesday is _____.

III. Listen and complete the sentences. 听录音补全句子。

1. Anna's phone number is _____.

2. Anna likes to play _____ with her friends.

3. Dave thinks playing ping-pong is _____ and easy.

4. Anna's _____ likes watching TV.

5. Anna's father is good at _____.

IV. Listen and finish the table. 听录音完成表格。

VISIT LONDON	
What to do:	visit (1) _____ museums
Where to stay:	a lovely hotel in the (2) _____ part of the city
Whom to go with:	my business (3) _____
When to stay:	from Saturday to (4) _____
How to go:	by (5) _____

长对话单选题

考试模块	时间	主题	内容	
			第5周目标	
	Day 1	休闲活动	A trip to Dublin	☐
	Day 2	休闲活动	考点锦囊及百变演练	☐
	Day 3	校园生活	An after-school music club	☐
Part 3 长对话 单选题	Day 4	校园生活	考点锦囊及百变演练	☐
	Day 5	环境设施	A new sports centre	☐
	Day 6	环境设施	考点锦囊及百变演练	☐
	Weekend	每周一练	基础训练及模拟训练	☐

Day 1　休闲活动·考场模拟

 考场模拟

Questions 11 – 15

For each question, choose the correct answer.

You will hear Robert talking to his friend, Laura, about a trip to Dublin.

11 Who has already decided to go with Robert?

  A family members   **B** colleagues   **C** tennis partners

12 They'll stay in

  A a university.   **B** a guest house.   **C** a hotel.

13 Laura must remember to take

  A a map.   **B** a camera.   **C** a coat.

14 Why does Laura like Dublin?

A The people are friendly.

B The buildings are interesting.

C The shops are beautiful.

15 Robert's excited about the trip to Dublin because

A he can't wait to go to the music festival.

B he loves the food there.

C he wants to go to a new art exhibition.

思路点拨

Step 1:【审题目，找关键】

1. **背景信息：** You will hear Robert talking to his friend, Laura, about a trip to Dublin.

   • 关键信息：人物—Robert和Laura；人物关系—friend；对话主题—trip

   • 文本翻译：你会听到罗伯特和他的朋友劳拉谈论去都柏林的旅行。

2. **题干及选项：**

   (11) [题干] Who has already decided to **go with Robert**?—谁已经决定和罗伯特一起去了？

   [选项]A family members—家庭成员；B colleagues—同事；C tennis partners—网球搭档

   [答案]选择 "**和罗伯特同行的人物身份**"。

   (12) [题干] They'll **stay in**—他们待在_____

   [选项]A a university—大学；B a guest house—家庭旅馆；C a hotel—宾馆

   [答案]选择 "**旅途中的住所**"。

   (13) [题干] **Laura** must remember to **take**—劳拉一定记得带_____

   [选项]A a map—地图；B a camera—照相机；C a coat—大衣

   [答案]选择 "**劳拉要带的物品**"。

   (14) [题干] Why does **Laura like** Dublin?—劳拉为什么喜欢都柏林？

   [选项]A The **people** are friendly.—（那里的）人们很友好；B The **buildings** are interesting.—（那里的）建筑很有趣；C The **shops** are beautiful.—（那里的）商店很漂亮

   [答案]选择 "**劳拉喜欢都柏林的原因**"。

(15) [题干] Robert's **excited about the trip** to Dublin **because**—罗伯特对都柏林之行感到兴奋是因为_____

[选项]A he can't wait to go to **the music festival**—他迫不及待要去音乐节；B he loves the **food** there—他喜欢那里的食物；C he wants to go to **a new art exhibition**—他想去看一个新的艺术展。

[答案]选择 "**罗伯特期待都柏林之行的原因**"。

Step 2:【听录音，选答案】

1. 听力原文：

M: Hi, Laura. Some of us are going for a weekend in Dublin this year. Are you free at the beginning of next month?

F: Yes, I'd love to come.

M: Great!

F: Who else is going?

M: I asked my cousins, but they're playing in a tennis competition—(11) so there'll be four of us from my office, and you.

F: Where are we staying?

M: I tried to book a guest-house. (12) It was full, but visitors can rent rooms in the university during the holidays. We'll do that—it's cheaper than a hotel.

F: Excellent. Are you taking your new camera?

M: Yes, some maps of the city too. (13) But you'll need a coat! It often rains.

F: OK!

M: Have you been before?

F: Yes! The centre's busy—the shops are always full of people! (14) My friends and I loved all the beautiful buildings—I really enjoyed learning about their history.

M: Yeah!

F: So, are you excited about the trip?

M: Yeah but it's a pity the music festival won't be on. (15) When I'm in Dublin I always have lots of fish—it's fantastic. There's a new art exhibition—you might like it, but I'm not interested.

F: Yeah, maybe!

2. **选择答案：**

(11) 当听到对话中女士的问句"Who else is going?"时要注意，以下就是介绍同行人的信息。首先Robert提到"my cousins"，该信息符合选项A "family members"，但后面转折连词"but"引出"他们要参加网球比赛"，即"无法同行"，故排除选项A。后面是so引出的表示"结果"的信息，"我办公室会有四个人，还有你（劳拉）"，根据"from my office"可推断出是他的"同事"，故B为正确答案。选项C在对话中仅出现了"tennis"，并未提及"partners"相关信息，故可排除。

(12) 题干中出现了关键信息"stay in"，对话中也提到了相关问题"Where are you staying?"首先提到了"guest house, I tried to..."（我尝试去），后面说"It was full"。即"订满了"，由此可知，虽然尝试定了，但是最后没成功，故排除B。后面又是转折连词"but"引出的信息"rent rooms in the university"，并且还提到"We'll do that"即"他们决定租大学里的房间"，故A为正确答案。最后继续补充选择大学的原因"it's cheaper than a hotel.（这比住宾馆要便宜。）"，他们也没有选择hotel，故选项C也可排除。

(13) 对话中提到要携带的物品时，女士（Laura）询问男士（Robert）"Are you taking your new camera?"根据男士肯定的回答"Yes, some maps of the city too."可知，Robert会带相机和城市地图；男士使用转折连词"but"继续说"You'll need a coat."，此处是嘱咐Laura要带一件大衣。故Laura要带的是选项C的大衣。

(14) 对话中Laura在描述Dublin这个地方时提到，"市中心熙熙攘攘的，商店里挤满了人"，"be full of"表示"充满……的"。后面Laura继续说"My friends and I loved all the beautiful buildings."。由此得知，Laura喜欢Dublin这个城市是因为"beautiful buildings"，三个选项中，B最符合文意。

(15) 题干中提到了短语"be excited about the trip"，对话中同样出现了该短语，Laura问Robert是否对旅行感到很兴奋。Robert回复时，用转折连词"but"引出了"music festival won't be on"即"音乐节不举行"，故排除A。接着提到"have lots of fish（吃很多鱼）"，并且用"fantastic（棒极了）"来形容鱼肉，"fish"就属于选项中的"food"一项，故B为正确答案。后面又提到"art exhibition, Robert"表示自己"not interested（不感兴趣）"，故可排除选项C。

【Answer key】

(11) B　　(12) A　　(13) C　　(14) B　　(15) B

Day 2　休闲活动·考点锦囊

 考点锦囊

1. 旅行通常会涉及如订票、预定住处、行程安排、收拾行李、游览景点等内容，常用单词或短语汇总如下。

旅行安排	
guest house 家庭旅馆	rent rooms 租房
book hotel 预订宾馆	check-in 登记处
flight 航程	guidebook 指南
guide 向导	journey 旅程，旅行
miss the train 错过火车	pack 打包
coach 长途汽车	student ticket 学生票
go on holiday 去度假	all over the world 全世界
be famous for 以……闻名	tourist information centre 旅游信息中心

2. 在长对话单选题中，常会遇到正确选项的表述在原文中是另外一种说法，此时就需要考生将有关信息建立起对应关系，以下是主题为"休闲活动"的同义转述的表达。

hard 困难的	difficult 困难的
towel 一条毛巾	something to dry yourself with 一些可以用来擦干的物品
sailing 航行	go out on a boat 坐船出去
opposite 在……对面	across the road 过马路
cycle 骑自行车	by bike 骑自行车
drink 饮料	a glass of juice 一杯果汁
have a sandwich 吃三明治	have a snack 吃零食
outside the shopping centre 在购物中心外面	near some shops 在一些商店附近
clear instructions 明确的指示	easy to understand 理解起来较为容易的
some water 一些水	something to drink 一些喝的东西
being with club members 和俱乐部成员在一起	spend time with the other players 花时间和其他成员在一起

百变演练

I. Complete the sentences with the words in the box. 用框中的单词补全句子。

> on   book   rent   full   pity

1. For some campsites, you have to phone and _____ before you go.

2. It's a _____ that you stopped learning the piano.

3. Is the party still _____ tonight or have they cancelled it?

4. They _____ rooms in their house to students.

5. My suitcase was _____ of books.

II. Listen and complete the sentence. 听录音补全句子。

1. Are you free at the _____ of next month?

2. Are you _____ about the trip?

3. I really enjoyed _____ _____ their history.

4. When I'm in Dublin I always have lots of fish—it's _____.

5. It's a pity the _____ _____ won't be on.

III. Listen and write T or F. 听录音判断正误。

(   ) 1. Laura's cousins will also be going to Dublin for the weekend.

(   ) 2. The guest-house that the man tried to book was available.

(   ) 3. Visitors can rent rooms in the university.

(   ) 4. It often rains in Dublin.

(   ) 5. Laura and her friends enjoyed learning about the history of Dublin's shops.

Day 3   校园生活・考场模拟

 考场模拟

Questions 11 – 15

For each question, choose the correct answer.

You will hear a teacher Martha talking to his student, Louis, about an after-school music club.

11 Louis's name isn't on the list because

  A he decided not to put his name on it.

  B he doesn't like music.

  C he didn't know about the list.

12 Miss Martha believes that Louis

  A may be able to be in the team.

  B won't be good enough for the team.

  C is the best player in the team.

13 Why can't Louis come to the after-school music club?

  A He has too much homework.

  B He has to go home with his sister.

  C His parents don't agree.

14 Louis's sister

  A doesn't like music at all.   **B** prefers music to studying.   **C** prefers studying to music.

15 If Louis wants to join the club, he has to tell his teacher

  A before next Tuesday.   **B** at this weekend.   **C** after next Monday.

 思路点拨

Step 1:【审题目，找关键】

1. **背景信息：** You will hear a teacher Martha talking to his student, Louis, about an after-school music club.

   • 关键信息：人物——Martha和Louis；人物关系——teacher and student；对话主题——after-school music club

   • 文本翻译：你会听到老师玛莎和他的学生路易斯谈论一个课后音乐俱乐部。

2. **题干及选项：**

(11) [题干] Louis's name **isn't on the list** because——路易斯的名字不在名单上是因为

   [选项]A he decided not to put his name on it——他决定不将自己的名字加入名单中；B he doesn't like music——他不喜欢音乐；C he didn't know about the list——他不知道有名单

[答案]选择"**路易斯没有报名音乐俱乐部的原因**"。

(12) [题干] Miss Martha believes that Louis—玛莎小姐认为路易斯_____

[选项]A may be able to be in the team—可能能够加入俱乐部；B won't be good enough for the team—还不够好；C is the best player in the team—是俱乐部中最好的演奏者

[答案]选择"**老师对路易斯的看法**"。

(13) [题干] Why can't Louis come to the after-school music club?—路易斯为什么不能参加课后音乐俱乐部？

[选项]A He has too much homework—作业太多；B He has to go home with his sister—他需要和妹妹一起回家；C His parents don't agree—他父母不同意

[答案]选择"**路易斯无法参加俱乐部的真实原因**"。

(14) [题干] Louis's sister—路易斯的妹妹_____

[选项]A doesn't like music at all—根本不喜欢音乐；B prefers music to studying—比起学习，更喜欢音乐；C prefers studying to music—比起音乐，更喜欢学习

[答案]选择"**路易斯妹妹的喜好**"。

(15) [题干] If Louis wants to join the club, he has to tell his teacher—如果路易斯想要加入俱乐部，他需要在_____告诉他的老师

[选项]A before next Tuesday—在下周二前；B at this weekend—在本周末；C after next Monday—在下周一之后

[答案]选择"**俱乐部最后截止时间**"。

Step 2:【听录音，选答案 】

1. 听力原文：

F: (11) Hello, Louis. I see your name isn't on the list for the after-school music club.

M: (11) Yes, I know that, Miss Martha.

F: (11) I thought you wanted to be in the school band.

M: (11) I do. I've been thinking about joining, (12) but I'm not sure if I am good enough.

F: (12) If you practise regularly, yes.

M: That's the problem. I can't come three times a week.

F: Is there too much homework?

M: (13) No, the homework is fine with me. I have to go home with my little sister. My parents both work, so they can't pick her up after school. And she's too young to travel alone.

F: I see. (14) <u>Is she interested in music?</u>

M: (14) <u>Not as much as studying.</u>

F: Do you think she might join the music club? Then you could still go home together.

M: That's a good idea. I think she might agree to come and watch but she won't take part.

F: OK. Then I think you could ask her if she wants to come.

M: Sure. So, it's not too late to add my name to the list?

F: (15) <u>Not if you do it before next Monday.</u> There are still three places left.

M: OK.

2. 选择答案：

(11) 对话开始时，老师就表明"路易斯的名字不在名单上"，路易斯回复说"Yes, I know that."。由此得知，路易斯知道此事，故排除选项C。老师接着说"我以为你想要加入校乐团"，路易斯的回复是"I do."，所以路易斯是喜欢音乐的，故选项B不正确。综合以上信息，路易斯没有报名，是自己的决定，故A为正确答案。

(12) 路易斯在回复俱乐部报名名单的问题时，说到"I've been thinking about joining, but I'm not sure if I am good enough."即"我一直在考虑加入，但我不确定自己是否足够好。"老师对此回复说"If you practise regularly, yes."。由此得知，老师认为路易斯只要练习的话，加入俱乐部是没有问题的。故选项A为正确答案。

(13) 对话中老师猜测路易斯没报名的原因是作业太多，路易斯回复说"作业不是问题"，后面给出了真正的原因"I have to go home with my little sister."。结合后面的详细信息可知，"路易斯的父母都要工作，无法在放学后接他的妹妹，他妹妹又太小，无法自己回家"，分析选项可知，正确答案为B。

(14) 题目询问"路易斯妹妹对音乐和学习的看法"，对话中老师问到"Is she interested in music?（她对音乐感兴趣吗？）"，路易斯的回复是"Not as much as studying."。短语"as much as"表示"和……一样多"，由此得知"路易斯的妹妹比较喜欢学习"。选项中短语"prefer A to B"表示"与B相比，更喜欢A"，故选项C为正确答案。

(15) 对话最后，路易斯询问老师"是否还可以将自己的名字增加到名单上"，老师回复说"Not if you do it before next Monday."。意思是"如果在下周一之前报名就还可以。"此句中的not指的是上句中的"not too late"。由此得知，最晚提交时间是下周一前，选项A给出的是"Tuesday（星期二）"，排除；选项B的"at this weekend"符合"下周一前"，为正确答案；选项C，对话中说的是"before"，不是"after"，故可排除。

【Answer key】

(11) A   (12) A   (13) B   (14) C   (15) B

Day 4 校园生活·考点锦囊

 **考点锦囊**

1. 考试中常会出现关于校园的内容，如课后俱乐部、学校比赛、学校课程等，常用单词或短语汇总如下。

校园生活	
art lesson 美术课	after-school club 课后俱乐部
school trip 学校旅行	have lessons 上课
be absent from school 缺课	miss class 缺课
prepare for 为……做准备	go back to school 返校
write down 写下	notes 笔记
attention 注意	correct 正确的
examination 考试	fail 考试不及格
hand in homework 交作业	library card 图书卡
make mistake 犯错	project 项目

2. 关于"校园及生活"常用到的同义转述表达如下。

presents 礼物	a little packet of sweets 一小包糖果
500 at the most 最多500	500 or less 500或以下
be good at 擅长……	be great at 擅长……
walk 步行	on foot 步行

health 健康	why people get ill and how doctors help them 人们为什么生病以及医生如何帮助他们
backpack 背包	put my school books in it 可以放进去我的课本
each person 每个人	everyone 每个人
start time 开始时间	begin at 开始于
put signs 贴些标示	put some posters 贴些海报
got more time to study 有更多的学习时间	give you longer to prepare for it 给你更长的时间去准备它

 百变演练

I. Complete the sentences with the correct form of the words in the box. 用框中单词的正确形式补全句子。

> agree   list   alone   band   practise

1. David _____ for more than a year to swim across the Cook Strait.

2. I don't like going out _____ at night.

3. Is your name on the _____?

4. Sam _____ to play the guitar on Thursday.

5. I play the keyboard in a _____.

II. Listen and write T or F. 听录音判断正误。

(　　) 1. Louis wants to join the after-school music club.

(　　) 2. Louis is confident in his musical abilities.

(　　) 3. Louis's parents are unable to pick up his little sister after school.

(　　) 4. Louis's little sister is more interested in music than him.

(　　) 5. Louis will ask his little sister if she wants to join the music club.

III. Translate. 翻译。

1. I thought you wanted to be in the school band.

2. Not if you do it before next Monday.

_____

3. She's too young to travel alone.

_____

4. I think you could ask her if she wants to come.

_____

5. There are still three places left.

_____

Day 5 环境设施·考场模拟

 考场模拟

Questions 11 – 15

For each question, choose the correct answer.

_____

You will hear Tony talking to his friend, Sue, about a new sports centre.

11 The new sports centre is

    A expensive   **B** large   **C** dark

12 What sport can't you do at the sports centre?

    A tennis   **B** badminton   **C** basketball

13 Sue has to pay

    A £102 a year   **B** £120 a year   **C** £80 a year

14 Which bus is better for going to the sports centre?

    A number 16   **B** number 18   **C** number 15

15 Tony and Sue are going to go to the sports centre next

    A Wednesday.   **B** Tuesday.   **C** Thursday.

🎧 思路点拨

Step 1:【审题目，找关键】

1. **背景信息：** You will hear Tony talking to his friend, Sue, about a new sports centre.

   • 关键信息：人物—Tony和Sue；人物关系—friend；对话主题—a new sports centre

   • 文本翻译：你会听到托尼和他的朋友苏谈论一个新的体育中心。

2. **题干及选项：**

   (11) [题干] The new sports centre is—新体育中心是_____

   [选项]A expensive—昂贵的；B large—大的；C dark—昏暗的

   [答案]选择"**新体育中心情况**"。

   (12) [题干] What sport can't you do at the sports centre?—在体育中心你不能进行哪项运动？

   [选项]A tennis—网球；B badminton—羽毛球；C basketball—篮球

   [答案]选择"**运动类型**"。

   (13) [题干] Sue has to pay—苏需要支付_____

   [选项]A £102 a year—每年102英镑；B £120 a year—每年120英镑；C £80 a year—每年80英镑

   [答案]选择"**金钱数字**"。

   (14) [题干] Which bus is better for going to the sports centre?—去体育中心乘坐哪辆公交车更好？

   [选项]A number 16—16路；B number 18—18路；C number 15—15路

   [答案]选择"**公交车线路数字**"。

   (15) [题干] Tony and Sue are going to go to the sports centre next—托尼和苏要在下周_____去体育中心。

   [选项]A Wednesday—星期三；B Tuesday—星期二；C Thursday—星期四

   [答案]选择"**去体育中心的时间(星期)**"。

Step 2:【听录音，选答案】

1. **听力原文：**

   M: Hello, Sue. Have you been to the new sports centre yet?

   F: No, Tony, where is it?

M: In Queen Street. You know, near Peace Square, behind the Molly Shopping Mall.

F: Oh. Is it good?

M: (11) Yes, it's big and light! You can do a lot of sports. I played badminton and basketball last weekend.

F: What about tennis?

M: (12) They haven't built the tennis courts yet, but they are planning to build one next year.

F: Is it expensive?

M: Not really, Sue. (13) It costs £120 per year if you're 14 to 18, and £80 if you're under 14.

F: (13) Oh, that's great, because I'm still 13.

M: Also, it stays open late until 10 o'clock on Monday, Wednesday, and Friday.

F: Oh, great. How did you get there?

M: (14) I took the number 18 bus. It's only 15 minutes from the bus station. Don't get bus 16 because you have to walk a long way. Would you like to go next week?

F: Sure. Any day except Tuesday.

M: (15) Well, why don't we go on Wednesday? Then we can stay late.

F: (15) Yes, OK. Let's meet after school.

2. **选择答案：**

(11) 题目询问对新的体育中心的评价，对话中Sue问Tony "Is it good?"，Tony用 "big and bright（又大又明亮）" 来形容，由此可排除选项C "dark（昏暗的）"，选项B "large" 与录音中 "big" 意思相同，故B为正确答案。关于体育中心的价格，Sue问Tony "Is it expensive?"，Tony的回复是 "Not really."，故可排除选项A。

(12) 对话在介绍体育中心的运动项目时，Sue问到了 "tennis（网球）"，Tony回复说 "They haven't built the tennis courts yet."，即 "他们还没有建网球场"，言外之意就是目前还没有办法打网球，故A为正确答案。选项B和C在对话中都有提到，Tony介绍时，提到自己上周末去打了羽毛球和篮球。

(13) 本题询问的是体育中心的价格，对话中提到 "It costs £120 per year if you're 14 to 18, and £80 if you're under 14."，即 "如果你在14到18岁，每年需要花费120英镑；如果年龄不到14岁，则花费80英镑"。下面Sue提到 "I'm still 13"，也就是不到14岁，所以Sue需要支付80英镑。故C为正确答案。

(14) Tony在介绍公交车线路时，先提到了自己乘坐的是 "number 18 bus"，然后提到

"bus 16"，但这时说的是"Don't get bus 16 because...（不要乘坐16路公交车）"，故排除选项A。对话中出现数字15，但表示的是车程是"15 minutes"，不是15路公交车，故选项C也可排除，正确答案是B。

(15) 两人在谈论到下周去体育中心的时间时，Sue先是说"Any day except Tuesday."，以此表示自己星期二没有时间，故可排除选项B。Tony建议"Why don't we go on Wednesday?"，Sue表示同意，故选项A为正确答案。

【Answer key】

(11) B   (12) A   (13) C   (14) B   (15) A

Day 6   环境设施·考点锦囊

 考点锦囊

1. 在听力考试中，听力内容有时也会涉及城市的环境设施，如超市、酒店、体育中心、图书馆、博物馆等等。

环境设施	
apartment 公寓	department store 百货商场
grocery store 杂货店	library 图书馆
post office 邮局	supermarket 超市
tennis court 网球场	college 大学
town centre 市中心	hotel 宾馆
town square 城市广场	railway station 火车站
swimming pool 游泳池	at the garage 在车库
car park 停车场	sports centre 体育中心
school playground 学校操场	movie theatre 电影院

2. 在听力对话单选题中，常会出现选项与原文中是同义或者反义，常见的同义及反义表述汇总如下。

同义转述		反义转述	
friendly 友好的	nice 友好的	surprised 惊讶	couldn't believe 不相信
pleased 高兴的	glad 高兴的	expensive 昂贵的	not cheap 不便宜
famous 著名的	well-known 众所周知的	boring 无聊	not very interesting 不是很有趣
good 好的	great 好的	hard 困难的	not easy 不同意的
scary 吓人的	a bit afraid 有点害怕	too dark 很黑	not bright enough 不够亮

3. 关于地点相关的同义转述如下。

garden 花园	next to the apple tree 在苹果树旁边
kitchen 厨房	next to the cooker 在炉子旁边
bedroom 卧室	next to my wardrobe 在我衣橱旁边
hall 大厅	the entrance by the front door 前门的入口
farm 农场	see the animals outside in the fresh air 在外面看动物

🎧 百变演练

I. Complete the sentences with the correct form of the words in the box. 用框中单词的正确形式补全句子。

> build   light   court   except   cost

1. A new basketball _____ has been built in the park.

2. The museum is open daily _____ Mondays.

3. It _____ four euros to swim at my favourite pool!

4. The houses are _____ out of local stone.

5. The new houses are big and _____.

II. Listen and write T or F. 听录音判断正误。

(   ) 1. The new sports centre is located near the Molly street.

(   ) 2. The sports centre offers a variety of sports activities.

(   ) 3. Tennis courts are already available at the sports centre.

(   ) 4. It costs £120 per year for people who are 14 to 18 years old.

(   ) 5. It takes 15 minutes to reach the sports centre from the bus station by bus number 18.

III. Choose correct words to complete the sentences. 选择正确单词补全句子。

1. A: How is Jason? Is he well?

    B: No, he has been _____ (ill / better) for many days.

2. A: The question wasn't very easy, was it?

    B: No, it was quite _____ (simple / difficult).

3. The bag is not big enough. It's too _____ (large / small).

Weekend 三

I. Complete the sentences with the correct form of the words in the box.
用框中单词的正确形式补全句子。

journey	pack	correct	attention
famous	book	ticket	coach

1. Neil is a _____ ice-hockey player and you can often see him on television.

2. If you don't pay _____ now, you'll get it all wrong later.

3. I've _____ a table at the restaurant for nine o'clock.

4. We're going to the airport by _____.

5. Bring a drink because the _____ to and from Gower Park takes an hour each way.

6. Put a tick before the answer that you think is _____.

7. You need to buy _____ before you travel on a bus or train.

8. I have to start _____ for my trip.

II. Read and choose the correct sentences to complete the conversation.
读一读，选择正确的句子补全对话。

(*Lee and Harry are talking in the school.*)

Lee: Look! There's a photo competition in the newspaper.

Harry: _____1_____ I'd like to have a try.

Lee: Well, you have to take a nice animal photo.

Harry: _____2_____ I can choose one.

Lee: No, it must be an animal that doesn't live with you.

Harry: I see._____3_____

Lee: Good idea! There are lots of animals there.

Harry: _____4_____

Lee: No, I don't. What about you?

Harry: _____ ___5_____ It doesn't work for a week.

Lee: Oh! Let's go to ask Leo for help.

A. Mine's broken.   B. I agree with you.

C. Sounds interesting!   D. I don't like animals.

E. Do you have a camera?   F. Let's go to the zoo.

G. I have many photos of my dogs!

III. Listen and choose the correct answer. 听录音选择正确答案。

(   ) 1. Why does the school plan to hold the competition?

A. To make students enjoy their school life.

B. To improve students' English speaking.

C. To encourage students to read more.

(   ) 2. Where will the competition be held?

A. In the school hall.   B. In the meeting room.   C. In the classroom.

(   ) 3. When will the competition be held?

A. On September 2nd.   B. On September 12th.   C. On September 20th.

(   ) 4. Who is Mrs. Jill?

A. A math teacher.   B. A head teacher.   C. An English teacher.

(   ) 5. What is the prize for the winners?

A. An English classic.   B. A free camping trip.   C. A trip to England.

Week 6 短对话/独白单选题

考试模块	时间	主题	内容	
			第6周目标	
Part 4 短对话/独白 单选题	Day 1	学校学习	Make less noise	☐
	Day 2	日常生活	Play a sport	☐
	Day 3	兴趣爱好	A photograph of a school playground	☐
	Day 4	休闲购物	Buy a bag	☐
	Day 5	天气情况	Wet weather	☐
	Weekend	每周一练	基础训练及模拟训练	☐

Day 1　学校学习

 考场模拟

Questions 16 – 20

For each question, choose the correct answer.

You will hear a teacher talking to her class.

What does the teacher want her class to do?

A work more quickly

B make less noise

C help each other more

思路点拨

Step 1:【审题目，找关键】

1. **背景信息：** You will hear a teacher talking to her class.
   - 关键信息：人物—teacher；事件—talking to her class
   - 文本翻译：你会听到一位老师在和她的学生讲话。

2. **题干：** What does the teacher want her class to do?
   - 关键信息：人物—teacher；事件—want her class to do；问题—what
   - 文本翻译：老师想要全班做什么？

3. **选项：**
   - 选项A：work more quickly（更迅速地工作）
   - 选项B：make less noise（少一些噪声）
   - 选项C：help each other more（更多地互相帮助）

Step 2:【听录音，选答案】

1. **听力原文：**

   F: I'm very pleased with your work. You're getting good marks and working together well. But you really must remember that other classes in rooms near us can't do their work if you shout at one another. Let's all show a bit more respect for other people—OK? Now—everyone has something to finish. Don't hurry, you have lots of time.

2. **选择答案：**
   - 老师在讲话开始时，对学生们的表现提出表扬，但紧接着出现转折连词"But"，此时需注意后面的是关键信息。"But you really must remember...OK?"此处老师想告诉学生"如果你们互相大喊大叫，邻班的同学们就无法做作业，让我们给他人多一些尊重"，由此得知，此处是要告诉同学们不要大吵大闹，即选项B，make less noise。
   - 老师开始提到"You're getting good marks and working together well."。由此可知，老师对学生们之间的互帮互助已经很满意了，故可排除选项C。
   - 老师最后提到"Don't hurry, you have lots of time."。由此得知，老师告诉学生"不要着急，你们有很多时间"，与选项A的work more quickly表达相反，故排除选项A。

【 Answer key 】B

🎧 百变演练

I. Listen and complete the sentences. 听录音补全句子。

1. I'm very _____ _____ your work.

2. You really must _____ that other classes in rooms near us can't do their work if you _____ _____ one another.

3. Let's all show a _____ more _____ for other people.

II. Complete the sentences with the words or phrases in the box. 用框中的单词补全句子。

| pleased | marks | hurry |

1. I got full _____ in the listening test.

2. We need to _____ or we'll be late for school.

3. She was very _____ with her exam results.

🎧 考点锦囊

在校园里，经常会接触各类通知，如布置作业、课堂纪律、比赛/活动通知、代课老师调配等。

校园通知

textbook page 教科书页码	maths homework 数学作业
write a story 写一个故事	school holidays 学校假期
phone number 电话号码	make noise 制造噪声
look forward to 期待着……	basketball match 篮球比赛
for a while 一段时间	instead 代替
spare time 空闲时间	sports day 运动会
at the moment 现在	term 学期
prepare for... 为……准备	detail 细节
geography 地理	chemistry 化学
information 信息	make a poster 制作海报

Day **2**　日常生活

 考场模拟

For each question, choose the correct answer.

You will hear two friends talking about their day.

What have they just done?

A They've been to a concert.

B They've had a meal.

C They've played a sport.

 思路点拨

Step 1:【审题目，找关键】

1. **背景信息：** You will hear two friends talking about their day.

   - 关键信息：人物—two friends；事件—talking about their day
   - 文本翻译：你会听到两位朋友在谈论他们的一天。

2. **题干：** What have they just done?

   - 关键信息：人物—they；事件—just have done；问题—what
   - 文本翻译：他们刚刚做了什么？

3. **选项：**

   - 选项A：They've been to a concert. （他们去听音乐会了。）
   - 选项B：They've had a meal. （他们吃了一顿饭。）
   - 选项C：They've played a sport. （他们进行了一项体育活动。）

Step 2:【听录音，选答案】

1. **听力原文：**

   M: That was great, wasn't it?

   F: Yes—everyone did really well today but I'm exhausted now and my legs really hurt! I'm going to go straight home and ask mum if I can have a pizza for dinner.

M: I'm going to lie on my bed and listen to music all evening.

F: Good idea! <u>We've done so much exercise today!</u>

2. **选择答案：**

- 根据录音中提到的 "exhausted（筋疲力尽的）"、"my legs really hurt（我的腿疼）" 以及对话最后提到的 "We've done so much exercise today（我们今天做了太多训练）"，可推断得知正确答案是体育运动，故选C。

- 对话中提到 "have a pizza for dinner"，看似与选项B有关联，但注意前面的信息 "I'm going to go straight home and ask mum"，由此得知，此处使用一般将来时，是说话者要直接回家并问妈妈是否可以晚饭吃比萨，故可排除B。

- 录音中还出现 "listen to music"，看似与选项A有关联，但同样，前面的信息 "I'm going to lie on my bed" 使用的也是一般将来时，此处是说男士说话者要回家躺在床上听音乐，故可以排除选项A。

【Answer key】C

🎧 百变演练

I. Listen and complete the sentences. 听录音补全句子。

1. Everyone did really well today but I'm _____ now and my legs really _____!

2. I'm going to _____ _____ home and ask mum if I can have a pizza for dinner.

3. I'm going to _____ _____ my bed and listen to music all evening.

II. Match the words in the box to the descriptions. 根据下面的描述匹配框中的单词。

| exhausted | straight | exercise |

1. very tired _____

2. physical activity _____

3. direct _____

考点锦囊

对话中形容 "疲惫" 时用到 "exhausted" 这个形容词，考试中还常考到的形容词如下。

形容词		
funny 有趣的	useful 有用的	long 长时间的
interesting 有趣的	boring 无聊的	tired 疲惫的
necessary 有必要的	noisy 吵闹的	worried 担心的
amazing 令人惊讶的	lucky 幸运的	lovely 令人愉快的
unlucky 不幸的	painful 疼痛的	bored 感到无聊的
bright 明亮的	hard 困难的	difficult 困难的

Day 3 兴趣爱好

 考场模拟

For each question, choose the correct answer.

You will hear two friends talking about a photograph.

What's the photograph of?

A a sports stadium

B a zoo

C a school playground

 思路点拨

Step 1:【审题目，找关键】

1. **背景信息：** You will hear two friends talking about a photograph.

   • 关键信息：人物—two friends；事件—talking about a photograph

   • 文本翻译：你会听到两个朋友在谈论一张照片。

2. **题干：** What's the photograph of?

   • 关键信息：物品—photograph

   • 文本翻译：这张照片是什么?

3. 选项：

- 选项A：a sports stadium（体育场）

- 选项B：a zoo（动物园）

- 选项C：a school playground（学校操场）

Step 2:【听录音，选答案】

1. **听力原文：**

M: What a great photo!

F: Thanks! They were all moving around so quickly—running and jumping about.

M: Is that a group of mothers over there?

F: Yes, and the little ones were all ready to go home. Their lessons were over for the day. It was raining, but they just wanted to run around after being indoors for so many hours.

2. **选择答案：**

- 录音开头就表明该对话的主题，即"a great photo（一张很棒的照片）"。

- 根据女士所说到的"the little ones were all ready to go home"以及上句提到的"a group of mothers"可知，照片中描述的人物是妈妈和孩子。

- 女士接着提到"他们一天的课程结束了。外面正在下雨，但是他们在室内待了好几个小时了（在教室上课），想（下课之后）到处跑一跑"，再结合最开始提到的照片内容"running and jumping about（跑来跑去，跳来跳去）"，可得知照片中发生的事情：

  人物——妈妈和孩子；事情——一些准备回家，一些在跑来跑去、跳来跳去；时间——一天课程结束；

  根据以上，可推断出选项中最符合的场景是a school playground（学校操场），故正确答案为C。

【Answer key】C

 百变演练

I. Translate. 翻译。

1. What a great photo!

2. Their lessons were over for the day.

_____

II. Listen and complete the sentences. 听录音补全句子。

1. They were all moving around so quickly—_____ and _____ about.

2. The little ones were all _____ to go home.

3. It was _____, but they just wanted to run around after being _____ for so many hours.

 考点锦囊

对话的听力考核中，常会涉及有关"兴趣爱好"的内容，如computer game（电脑游戏）、go swimming（去游泳）、reading（阅读）等。

兴趣爱好		
hobby 兴趣	**collect** 收集	**video game** 电子游戏
music 音乐	**musician** 音乐家	**art equipment** 美术用具
photograph 摄影；照片	**camera** 相机	**be interested in** 对……感兴趣
barbecue 户外烧烤	**get bored** 觉得无聊	**game website** 游戏网站
computer 电脑	**fan** 迷	**draw** 画画

Day 4　休闲购物

考场模拟

For each question, choose the correct answer.

_____

You will hear a girl, Lara, talking about shopping.

Why did Lara buy the bag?

A The size was right.

B The price was right.

C The colour was right.

 思路点拨

Step 1:【审题目，找关键】

1. **背景信息：** You will hear a girl, Lara, talking about shopping.
   - 关键信息：人物—Lara；事件—talking about shopping
   - 文本翻译：你会听到一个女孩劳拉在谈论购物。

2. **题干：** Why did Lara buy the bag?
   - 关键信息：人物—Lara；事件—buy the bag；问题—why
   - 文本翻译：劳拉为什么买这个包？

3. **选项：**
   - 选项A：The size was right.（尺寸合适。）
   - 选项B：The price was right.（价格合适。）
   - 选项C：The colour was right.（颜色合适。）

Step 2:【听录音，选答案】

1. **听力原文：**

   M: Let's see your new bag, Lara. Oh, why did you get that one? You wanted a pale colour.

   F: I know! But this was the only one in the shop that was big enough for all my school stuff!

   M: Right. Well, it looks good. Did it cost a lot?

   F: Yeah, much too much. Mum had to lend me some money.

2. **选择答案：**

   - 对话开始朋友问Lara "Oh, why did you get that one? You wanted a pale colour.（为什么买那个包？你不是想要一个浅色的吗？）"。由此推断，Lara并不是因为颜色而买，故排除选项C。

   - Lara回复说 "But this was the only one in the shop that was big enough for all my school stuff."。此处使用了转折连词but，考生需注意，后面的信息为Lara买这个包的真正理由，即 "这个包是店里唯一一个，它足够大可以装得下我所有的学校用品"，此处的 "big enough" 所指代的就是 "size"，故A为正确答案。

   - 对话最后，朋友问Lara "Did it cost a lot?（这个包贵吗？）"，Lara回复说 "much too much"，即"花了很多钱"，由此推断，价格并不合适，故可排除选项B。

【Answer key】A

 百变演练

I. Match the words in the box to the descriptions. 根据下面的描述匹配框中的单词。

> enough   stuff   pale

1. very light-coloured　　　　　　　　　_____

2. as much as necessary　　　　　　　_____

3. things　　　　　　　　　　　　　　_____

II. Listen and complete the sentences. 听录音补全句子。

1. This was the _____ one in the shop that was big enough for all my _____ _____.

2. Mum had to _____ me some money.

 考点锦囊

在听到涉及"购物"的相关内容时，经常需要考生针对购买的物品、颜色、尺寸、价格等信息做出选择和判断。

休闲购物		
size 尺寸	price 价格	go for 挑选
colour 颜色	bill 账单	pale colour 浅色
shop assistant 店员	try on 试穿	advertisement 广告
receipt 收据	credit card 信用卡	school stuff 学校用品
get a discount 打折	special offer 特价	choose 选择
save money 省钱	magazine 杂志	shopping list 购物清单

Day 5　天气情况

 考场模拟

For each question, choose the correct answer.

You will hear a man talking to his daughter before she goes out.

What's the weather like today?

A It's cold.

B It's wet.

C It's sunny.

 思路点拨

Step 1:【审题目，找关键】

1. **背景信息：** You will hear a man talking to his daughter before she goes out.

   ● 关键信息：人物—a man和his daughter；事件—talking；时间—before she goes out

   ● 文本翻译：你会听到一个男士在女儿出门前和她说话。

2. **题干：** What's the weather like today?

   ● 关键信息：话题—weather；时间—today

   ● 文本翻译：今天天气怎么样？

3. **选项：**

   ● 选项A：It's cold.（寒冷。）

   ● 选项B：It's wet.（下雨。）

   ● 选项C：It's sunny.（晴朗。）

Step 2:【听录音，选答案】

1. **听力原文：**

   M: Have you looked out of the window this morning, Kate?

   F: Why, Dad? What do you mean?

   M: You won't need your warm coat today. The weather forecast says the temperature's definitely going to be higher than yesterday.

F: Great. I'm going to the city centre with Diana this morning.

M: But take an umbrella because it's just starting to rain.

F: All right, no problem.

2. **选择答案：**

- 对话中爸爸提醒Kate "But take an umbrella because it's just starting to rain." 。由此得知，此时刚刚开始下雨，由此推断，天气应是"下雨的"，"wet"除了表示"潮湿的"意思，也可表达"下雨的"，故选B。

- 对话中提到 "The weather forecast says the temperature's definitely going to be higher than yesterday.（天气预报说温度一定比昨天要高）"，并未明确说"cold"和"sunny"，故可排除选项A和C。

【 Answer key 】B

百变演练

I. Listen and complete the sentences. 听录音补全句子。

1. Have you _____ _____ _____ the window this morning?

2. The _____ forecast says the _____ is definitely going to be _____ than yesterday.

3. Take an _____ because it's just _____ to rain.

II. Complete the sentences with the words in the box. 用框中的单词补全句子。

> forecast   high   mean

1. What does this word _____?

2. In summer, the temperatures can be as _____ as 40°C.

3. The weather _____ said it was going to be hot and sunny tomorrow.

考点锦囊

对话的听力考核中，有时会涉及有关"天气"的内容，如根据天气增减衣物、出行提醒等，与其相关的常用表达如下。

天气情况		
cloud 云	**cloudy** 多云的	**take an umbrella** 带把伞
cool 凉爽的	**warm** 暖和的	**rain** 雨；下雨
fog 雾	**foggy** 有雾的	**storm** 暴风雨
hot 热的	**cold** 寒冷的	**thunderstorm** 雷暴
snow 雪；下雪	**snowy** 雪多的	**wet** 下雨的；潮湿的
sunny 阳光充足的	**wind** 风	**dry** 干的

Weekend 三

I. Read the descriptions and choose the correct words from the box. 阅读描述，从框中选择正确的单词。

| discount | stadium | bored | foggy | information | storm |

1. It's a message received and understood. _____

2. a reduction in the usual price _____

3. very bad weather with strong winds and heavy rain _____

4. feel uninterested _____

5. You cannot see clearly in this kind of weather condition. _____

6. It is a large sports ground. _____

II. Read the sentences and choose the correct answer. 阅读句子并选择正确的答案。

1. The film wasn't interesting—we all thought it was _____.

    A. boring   B. funny   C. amazing

2. Could you please tell me your _____?

    A. flat   B. house   C. address

3. The class was so _____ —I couldn't hear what the teacher was saying.

   A. quiet   B. noisy   C. calm

4. I play the violin in a band. I am a _____.

   A. musician   B. cook   C. doctor

5. It's cold outside. So you have to wear your _____.

   A. skirt   B. coat   C. umbrella

III. Read and choose the correct sentences to complete the conversation.
读一读，选择正确的句子补全对话。

A: Tomorrow is my sister's birthday. I want to give her a nice present.

B: _____ 1 _____

A: I'm not sure. Do you have any good ideas?

B: Let me see. _____ 2 _____

A: Yes. She thinks reading is interesting.

B: Well, you can buy her some books.

A: _____ 3 _____ Thank you.

B: That's OK. I want to give her a present too. _____ 4 _____

A: Yes, she loves them very much.

B: _____ 5 _____

A: Orange and purple.

B: OK, I see.

> A. What does she like?   B. What colour does she like?
>
> C. What do you want to give her?   D. Does she like flowers?
>
> E. That's a great idea.   F. Does she like reading?
>
> G. What does she do?

IV. Listen the conversation and choose the correct answer. 听对话选择正确
答案。

1. You'll hear the son and mother talking about what to drink.

   What does the boy decide to drink at last?

   A. Juice.   B. Yogurt.   C. Coffee.

2. You'll hear two friends talking about the weekend plan.

   What will Lisa do this weekend?

   A. Have a picnic.   B. Have a test.   C. Study English.

3. You'll hear a man and a shop assistant talking about the clothes price.

   How much should the man pay?

   A. $5   B.$9   C. $4.5

4. You'll hear a man and a woman talking together.

   Where are they?

   A. In a school.   B. In a hospital.   C. At home.

5. You will hear a woman talking on the phone.

   Why's she upset?

   A. Her train was delayed.   B. She's lost her wallet.   C. She's broken her glasses.

		第7周目标		
考试模块	时间	主题	内容	
Part 5 信息匹配题	Day 1	聚会庆祝	What will each person bring to the party?	☐
	Day 2	聚会庆祝	考点锦囊及百变演练	☐
	Day 3	校园活动	Where did they and their friends go to draw their pictures?	☐
	Day 4	校园活动	考点锦囊及百变演练	☐
	Day 5	日常交流	What jobs does each person want to do?	☐
	Day 6	日常交流	考点锦囊及百变演练	☐
	Weekend	每周一练	基础训练及模拟训练	☐

Day 1　聚会庆祝·考场模拟

 考场模拟

Questions 21 – 25

For each question, choose the correct answer.

You will hear Simon talking to Maria about a party.

What will each person bring to the party?

Example:

0　　Maria　　　　　B

People			Food
21	Barbara	☐	A bread

22	Simon	☐	B cake
			C cheese
23	Anita	☐	D chicken
24	Peter	☐	E fish
			F fruit
25	Michael	☐	G ice cream
			H salad

 ## 思路点拨

Step 1:【审题目，找关键】

1. **背景信息：** You will hear Simon talking to Maria about a party.

   - 关键信息：人物—Simon和Maria；事件—a party
   - 文本翻译：你会听到西蒙和玛丽亚谈论一个聚会。

2. **题干：** What will each person bring to the party?

   - 关键信息：人物—each person；事件—bring to the party
   - 文本翻译：每个人会给聚会带什么？

3. **选项：**

   - 左列：人物5个—Barbara；Simon；Anita；Peter；Michael
   - 右列：食物8项—bread（面包）；cake（蛋糕）；cheese（奶酪）；chicken（鸡肉）；fish（鱼）；fruit（水果）；ice cream（冰激凌）；salad（沙拉）

Step 2:【听录音，选答案】

1. **听力原文：**

   M: Are you nearly ready for your birthday party on Saturday, Maria?

   F: (22) I think so, Simon. I've made a cake and my friends are bringing the other food.

   M: That's a good idea.

   F: (21) Barbara's going to bring some oranges and grapes.

   M: (22) And I'll bring some bread and cheese from the market if you like. Everyone gets hungry at parties, don't they?

   F: Thanks, Simon. (22)&(23) But you don't need to bring bread because Anita's bringing that. She wanted to bring ice cream but I think the weather's too cold!

M: Mm, it is. (24) Perhaps Peter can help. He likes cooking, doesn't he?

F: (24) Yes, he emailed me and asked me to choose roast chicken or fish. I chose chicken because it's more popular than fish. What do you think?

M: That sounds great! (25) What's Michael bringing—he's coming, isn't he?

F: Yes, he loves parties! (25) I telephoned him and he's going to make a big bowl of sliced tomatoes and onions.

M: Lovely!

2. **选择答案：**

(21) Barbara-F。根据人物Barbara，可以定位到原文中"Barbara's going to bring some oranges and grapes."，句中的"oranges（橘子）"和"grapes（葡萄）"都属于水果，所以Barbara要带的东西是"fruit"，故选F。

(22) Simon-C。根据对话开头可知，对话中的女士是Maria，男士是Simon。所以当男士说"I'll bring some bread and cheese from the market."时，可知此处提到Simon要带的是"bread（面包）"和"cheese（奶酪）"；但是下面Maria又提到"you don't need to bring bread."。由此可知，Simon只需要带"cheese"即可，故选C。

(23) Anita-A。对话中在提到Anita时说"But you don't need to bring bread because Anita's bringing that."。由此可知，Anita要带的是"bread（面包）"，故选A。需要注意，虽然后面紧接着提到"She wanted to bring ice cream but I think the weather's too cold.（她本想带冰激凌，但是觉得天气太冷了。）"，考生在听时，一定要注意转折连词"but"后面的信息。

(24) Peter-D。对话中男士首先提到了Peter，然后女士说"He emailed me and asked me to choose roast chicken or fish.（他给我发了一封电子邮件，让我选择烤鸡或烤鱼。）"。故Peter本想选择的东西是"chicken"或"fish"。但女士接着说"I chose chicken because it's more popular than fish.（我选择了鸡肉是因为它比鱼更受欢迎。）"。由此可知，女士替Peter做出了选择，即"chicken"，故选D。

(25) Michael-H。对话中男士问"What's Michael bringing?（迈克尔带什么？）"，女士在回答时提到"a big bowl of sliced tomatoes and onions（一大碗切好的西红柿和洋葱）"，即选项中的salad（沙拉），故选H。

Day 2 聚会庆祝·考点锦囊

 考点锦囊

在考试中，选项中的内容通常不会1:1直接出现在原文中，而是会以"同义转述"的方式呈现，以下是真题中曾经出现过的部分表达。

题目表达	原文表达
sport 运动	exercise 运动
fruit 水果	oranges and grapes 橘子和葡萄
food 食物	snacks 小吃；dishes 菜肴
family 家庭	aunt and uncle 阿姨和叔叔
friendly 友好的	nice 友好的
juice 果汁	something to drink 一些喝的东西
price 价格	discount 折扣
neighbour 邻居	the woman who lives next door 住在隔壁的女人
sports equipment 运动器材	net 球网；ball 球；bat 球拍
sleep a lot 多睡觉	go to bed early 早睡
art equipment 美术用具	pencils and paints 铅笔和颜料
photography 摄影	taking pictures 拍照
swimming 游泳	spend time at the pool 在游泳池消磨时间
poster 海报	something to put on my bedroom wall 放在我卧室墙上的东西
scarf 围巾	keep me warm in winter 在冬天让我保暖
visit grandparents 看望祖父母	stay with his granny and grandad 和他的奶奶和爷爷待在一起

百变演练

I. Listen and complete the sentences. 听录音补全句子。

1. Barbara's going to bring some _____ and _____.

2. Everyone gets _____ at parties, don't they?

3. I _____ chicken _____ it's more popular than fish.

4. What's Michael _____ —he's coming, isn't he?

5. I _____ him and he's going to make a big _____ of sliced tomatoes and onions.

II. Complete the sentences with the words in the box. 用框中的单词补全句子。

| cook | ready | choose | nearly | popular |

1. She's _____ as tall as her father now.

2. Everything's packed, and we're _____ to leave.

3. Tonight Mum is going to _____ Chinese food for us.

4. You _____ —I can't decide.

5. Ashley Trent, one of our most _____ young actors, is now filming College Rap.

III. Listen and write T or F. 听录音判断正误。

(   ) 1. Maria has already made all the food for her birthday party.

(   ) 2. Barbara is bringing oranges and grapes to the party.

(   ) 3. Simon will bring bread and cheese to the party.

(   ) 4. Anita will bring ice cream to the party.

(   ) 5. Peter will help with cooking at the party.

Day 3   校园活动 · 考场模拟

 考场模拟

Questions 21 – 25

For each question, choose the correct answer.

You will hear Ann talking to Paul about a school art lesson.

Where did they and their friends go to draw their pictures?

Example:

0	Paul	E

People			Places
21	Ann		**A** museum
22	Andrew		**B** restaurant
			C sea
23	Grace		**D** clothes shop
24	Colin		**E** sports centre
			F bookshop
25	Marina		**G** cafe
			H market

🎧 思路点拨

Step 1:【审题目，找关键】

1. **背景信息：** You will hear Ann talking to Paul about a school art lesson.

   - 关键信息：人物—Ann和Paul；事件—a school art lesson
   - 文本翻译：你会听到安和保罗谈论学校的美术课。

2. **题干：** Where did they and their friends go to draw their pictures?

   - 关键信息：人物—they and their friends；事件—draw their pictures
   - 文本翻译：他们和他们的朋友去哪里画画了？

3. **选项：**

   - 左列：人物5个—Ann；Andrew；Grace；Colin；Marina
   - 右列：地点8项—museum（博物馆）；restaurant（餐厅）；sea（大海）；clothes shop（服装店）；sports centre（体育中心）；bookshop（书店）；cafe（咖啡馆）；market（市场）

Step 2:【听录音，选答案】

1. **听力原文：**

   M: The art class this week was really interesting, Ann. I really enjoyed it.

F: So did I, Paul. I liked drawing different places or buildings of this city. Is this your picture of the park?

M: Yes. What did you draw?

F: (21) I couldn't decide between the museum and the market. At last I drew a picture of people selling fruit and vegetables. (22) Do you know what Andrew drew?

M: Yes, I met him in a bookshop after the lesson. (22) His picture was of some people in the cafe reading books.

F: (23) I know Grace loves drawing water. Did she go to the sea?

M: (23) Well, she went to the sports centre and drew some people swimming. (24) What did Colin draw? You know, he is the best artist.

F: (24) We were walking to the market together but then he saw someone buying clothes in a shop and he stopped to draw that. (25) What about Marina?

M: (25) I saw her in Main Street sitting at a table having a sandwich. She was drawing a waitress talking to a lady.

F: What an interesting art lesson!

2. 选择答案:

(21) Ann-H。通过对话开头便可知，Ann就是对话中说话的女士。当男士Paul问到Ann画了什么时，Ann说 "I couldn't decide between the museum and the market."，根据本句可将Ann画画的地址限定为 "museum" 和 "market"。她紧接着继续说 "At last I drew a picture of people selling fruit and vegetables.（最后我画了一幅卖水果和蔬菜的人的画。）"。句中 "sell fruit and vegetables" 发生的场景就是上面提到的market，故选H。

(22) Andrew-G。女士问男士 "Do you know what Andrew drew?" 接下来男士描述的就是Andrew画画的内容 "His picture was of some people in the cafe reading books.（他的画是一些人在咖啡馆看书。）"。由此可知，Andrew是在 "cafe" 画画。此处容易混淆的是 "bookshop"，男士一开始说 "I met him in a bookshop after the lesson."，男士只是在 "bookshop" 见到了Andrew，并不代表Andrew是在书店画的画。故正确答案为G。

(23) Grace-E。女士提到 "Grace loves drawing water."，即Grace喜欢画水。男士回复说 "She went to the sports centre and drew some people swimming."。由此可知Grace去

了体育中心画人们游泳了，故选E。

(24) Colin-D。男士询问女士"What did Colin draw?"女士回答说"We were walking to the market together but then he saw someone buying clothes in a shop and he stopped to draw that."。句中先提到了"market"，但后面紧接着用了转折连词"but"，根据后面的信息"他看见有人在商店里买衣服，于是他停下来画了这幅画"可知Colin最终是去了服装店画画，故选D。

(25) Marina-B。对话最后提到了Marina，根据男士描述的信息中的"sitting at a table having a sandwich（坐在桌子旁吃三明治）"和"a waitress talking to a lady（一个女服务员在和一位女士说话）"可推断出，该场景应发生在餐厅里，故选B。

Day 4　校园活动·考点锦囊

 考点锦囊

1. 在有关校园的信息匹配题中，常会涉及如学校郊游、课程安排、运动会项目、学校演出张贴海报等相关话题，选项中涉及的类别有places（地点）、help with sth.（帮助做的事情）、things to bring（要带的东西）、activities（活动）或sports（运动）等。

地点	
apartment building 公寓楼	cafe 咖啡馆
large store 大型商店	library 图书馆
museum 博物馆	station 车站
post office 邮局	sports centre 体育中心
supermarket 超市	bookshop 书店

要带的东西	
board game 棋盘游戏	camera 照相机
drum 鼓	guitar 吉他
pencils and paints 铅笔和颜料	picnic bag 野餐包
quiz 小测验	sports equipment 运动器材

2. 出现在卷面中的选项内容通常在录音中是另外一种表述方式。

picnic bag 野餐包	something to carry all the stuff to eat 能带着所有吃的东西的物品
quiz 小测验	something where everyone takes part, answering questions in teams 每个人都参与其中，在团队中回答问题
library 图书馆	place where we can borrow books 借书的地方
big shop 大商店	large store 大商店
flat 公寓	apartment 公寓
laptop 笔记本电脑	computer 电脑

 百变演练

I. Match the words and phrase in the box to the sentences or questions. 根据下面的句子或问题匹配框中的单词和短语。

> sports centre　　market　　museum　　restaurant　　bookshop

1. I'd like a kilo of potatoes. _____

2. What time does the tennis class start? _____

3. I'll have a cheese hamburger, please. _____

4. The paintings were discovered in China in 1643. _____

5. What type of books are you interested in? _____

II. Listen and complete the sentences. 听录音补全句子。

1. The art class this week was really interesting, Ann. I really _____ it.

2. I couldn't _____ between the museum and the market.

3. We were _____ to the market together.

4. I saw her in Main Street _____ at a table having a sandwich.

5. At last I _____ a picture of people _____ fruit and vegetables.

III. Listen and write T or F. 听录音判断正误。

(　　) 1. Paul and Ann enjoyed their art class this week.

(　　) 2. Paul drew a picture of the museum.

(   ) 3. Andrew's picture was of some people reading books in a cafe.

(   ) 4. Colin saw someone buying clothes in a market and stopped to draw that.

Day 5　日常交流 · 考场模拟

🎧 考场模拟

Questions 21 – 25

For each question, choose the correct answer.

You will hear Eason talking to his sister Suzie about the jobs his classmates want to do.

What jobs does each person want to do?

Example:

0	Eason	A

People			Jobs
21	David	☐	**A** artist
22	Tanya	☐	**B** teacher
			C dentist
23	Julie	☐	**D** journalist
24	Eric	☐	**E** pilot
			F mechanic
25	Ricky	☐	**G** actor
			H engineer

🎧 思路点拨

Step 1:【审题目，找关键】

1. **背景信息：** You will hear Eason talking to his sister Suzie about the jobs his classmates want to do.

- 关键信息：人物—Eason和Suzie；事件—the jobs
- 文本翻译：你会听到伊森和他的姐姐苏茜谈论他的同学想要做的工作。

2. **题干：** What **jobs** does **each person want to do**?

- 关键信息：人物—each person；事件—jobs, want to do
- 文本翻译：每个人都想做什么工作？

3. **选项：**

- 左列：人物5个—David；Tanya；Julie；Eric；Ricky
- 右列：职业8项—artist（艺术家）；teacher（老师）；dentist（牙医）；journalist（记者）；pilot（飞行员）；mechanic（机修工）；actor（演员）；engineer（工程师）

Step 2：【听录音，选答案】

1. **听力原文：**

M: Suzie, we talked about future jobs in school today, which was really interesting.

F: So Eason, what do you want to do?

M: I love paintings and drawings. So I want to be an artist.

F: Sound great! (21) What is David's dream job?

M: (21) He loves flying, so he'd like to fly planes and travel around the world.

F: Oh, really! Amazing! Then let me guess, Tanya wants to be a teacher, doesn't she?

M: She wanted to be a teacher but now she wants to work at the hospital. You know her father is a doctor there, (22) and she wants to help people with their teeth.

F: That sounds like a good job too. (23) And Julie?

M: She likes reading and writing, so (23) she wants to write stories or articles for newspapers.

F: She'll be good at that. (24)What about Eric?

M: (24) He's always helping his dad repair cars at the weekend. So that's what he wants to do.

F: Cool! Does Ricky know what he wants to do?

M: Oh, handsome Ricky! He acted well in the school play. (25) But he wants to design and build machines in the future.

F: Wow! That's impressive.

2. **选择答案：**

(21) David-E。对话中在谈到David时说"He loves flying, so he'd like to fly planes and

---

travel around the world." 。根据句中的 "flying" 以及 "fly planes" 可知David想要做的事情是和 "开飞机" 相关的，选项中 "pilot（飞行员）" 符合，故选E。

(22) Tanya-C。在谈到Tanya时，首先是女士提到的 "Tanya wants to be a teacher, doesn't she?"，接下来男士回复说 "but now she wants to work at the hospital"，即现在她想在医院工作，所以可排除 "老师"。后面又提到她的父亲是医生 "she wants to help people with their teeth"，结合 "在医院工作" 以及 "帮助别人处理牙齿" 可知Tanya想做的是 "dentist（牙医）"。

(23) Julie-D。对话中在谈到Julie时，提到 "She likes reading and writing, so she wants to write stories or articles for newspapers.（她喜欢阅读和写作，所以她想为报纸写故事或文章。）。" 根据此句可得知，Julie想做的是journalist（记者）的职业，故选D。

(24) Eric-F。对话中在谈到Eric时提到 "He's always helping his dad repair cars at the weekend. So that's what he wants to do.（他常常在周末帮助他的父亲修车。所以这就是他想要做的。）"。选项中，"repair cars" 的职业是 "mechanic（机修工）"。故选F。

(25) Ricky-H。对话中在谈到Ricky时提到 "But he wants to design and build machines in the future.（但他想在未来设计和制造机器。）" 选项中，与 "design and build machines" 相匹配的职业是 "engineer（工程师）"，故选H。

Day 6 　日常交流·考点锦囊

🎧 考点锦囊

1. 在听力考试中，常会涉及与工作职业相关的话题，如家人的工作、同学朋友未来想从事的职业、暑期兼职工作等。通常职业的内容在文中不会直接给出，会以 "同义转述" 的方式呈现。

Jobs	
职业	工作描述
artist 艺术家	**do paintings and drawings** 画画
mechanic 机修师	**repair cars or machines** 修理汽车或机器

续表

dentist 牙医	help people with their teeth 帮助人们修理牙齿
cook 厨师	prepare food in a restaurant 在餐厅准备食物
actor 演员	play a character in a film or play 在电影或戏剧中扮演角色
pilot 飞行员	fly aircraft 飞行飞机
boss 老板	always tell you what to do at work 总是告诉你工作中应该做什么
journalist 记者	write news stories for newspapers 为报纸写新闻故事
receptionist 接待员	greet visitors and answer the phone 接待访客和接听电话
tour guide 导游	show visitors around a place 带游客参观一个地方

2. 在信息匹配题中，录音对话中常听到的高频句型如下。

- What about...? ……呢？/……怎么样？

  What about your sister? 你的妹妹呢？

- Why not...? 为什么不……？

  Why not put posters in different places around town? 为什么不在城里的不同地方张贴海报呢？

- What did sb. give you? 某人给了你什么？

  What did your uncle give you? 你的叔叔给你什么了？

- sb. offered to do... 某人主动提出做……

  The kids offered to do the dishes. 孩子们主动提出要洗碗。

🎧 百变演练

I. Match the words in the box to the descriptions. 根据下面的句子匹配框中的单词。

mechanic	artist	actor	dentist	pilot

1. This person does paintings and drawings. _____

2. This person helps people with their teeth. _____

3. This person flies aircraft. _____

4. This person repairs cars or machines. _____

5. This person plays a character in a film. _____

II. Listen and complete the sentences. 听录音补全句子。

1. I love _____ and drawings.

2. He loves flying, so he'd like to fly planes and _____ _____ the world.

3. She wanted to be a teacher but now she wants to work at the _____ .

4. She wants to write stories or _____ for newspapers.

5. He wants to design and build _____ in the future.

III. Listen and write T or F. 听录音判断正误。

( ) 1. Eason wants to be an artist.

( ) 2. Tanya wants to be a teacher.

( ) 3. Tanya wants to work at the hospital.

( ) 4. Julie wants to write stories for newspapers.

( ) 5. Ricky wants to be an actor.

Weekend 三

I. Complete the sentences with the correct form of the words in the box.
用框中单词的正确形式补全句子。

bring	enjoy	cheese	decide	salad	repair	email	build

1. Would you like a slice of _____ with your bread?

2. I'd like a _____ of tomato, onion and cucumber.

3. I'll see if Jason will _____ her guitar to the party.

4. You can contact us by _____ or fax.

5. He can't _____ whether to buy it.

6. The car was broken and it is difficult to _____ .

7. They want to _____ a bridge across the river.

8. If you _____ watching films at home, you may need to rent a video.

II. Read the sentences and choose the correct answer. 阅读句子并选择正确的答案。

1. I have a toothache. I think I'd better go to see a _____.

   A. dentist   B. teacher   C. boss

2. I'm famous because I've acted in many films. I'm an _____.

   A. engineer   B. artist   C. actor

3. I'm so hungry. Do you know the nearest _____?

   A. museum   B. restaurant   C. bank

4. She's thirsty and wants something to drink. You can give her _____.

   A. a slice of cheese   B. a glass of juice   C. a bowl of salad

5. Jane's mother is a _____. She writes wonderful articles for newspapers and magazines.

   A. journalist   B. mechanic   C. receptionist

III. Look at the table，read the sentences and write T or F. 根据表格并阅读句子，判断正误。

	Singing	Sailing	Playing computer games	Snowboarding
Amy	☺☺	☺	☺☺☺	☹
Jason	☹	☺☺	☺	☺
Liam	☺	☺☺	☹	☹
Olivia	☹	☹	☺☺	☺☺☺

(   ) 1. Liam likes playing computer games.

(   ) 2. Jason thinks sailing is more interesting than snowboarding.

(   ) 3. Olivia prefers playing computer games to snowboarding.

(   ) 4. Amy enjoys singing and snowboarding.

(   ) 5. Liam doesn't like playing computer games and snowboarding.

(   ) 6. Jason prefers sailing to playing computer games.

(   ) 7. Olivia thinks singing is boring.

(   ) 8. Jason and Olivia are both like snowboarding.

IV. Listen and choose the correct answer. 听录音选择正确的答案。

You will hear Amy talking to her friend about her birthday party.

What birthday present does each person give her?

People			Presents
1	Mum	☐	A keyboard
2	Grandpa	☐	B sweater
			C computer
3	Dad	☐	D mobile phone
4	Brother	☐	E photo album
			F camera
5	Grandma	☐	G T-shirt
			H gloves

8

Mock Test 模拟考试

第8周目标				
考试模块	时间	主题	内容	
Mock Test 模拟考试	Day 1	Part 1 短对话图片单选题	听力模拟训练2套	☐
	Day 2	Part 2 独白摘要题	听力模拟训练2套	☐
	Day 3	Part 3 长对话单选题	听力模拟训练2套	☐
	Day 4	Part 4 短对话/独白单选题	听力模拟训练2套	☐
	Day 5	Part 5信息匹配题	听力模拟训练2套	☐
		答案解析	听力模拟训练解析（Day 1-5）	☐

Day 1　短对话图片单选题

Test 1

Questions 1-5

For each question, choose the correct picture.

---

1 What's the name of the new Spanish teacher?

A

B

C

2 What is Josh doing tomorrow?

A

B

C

3 How much are the bananas?

 A B C

4 When's Robbie's mum's birthday?

 A B C

5 What does the boy order?

 A 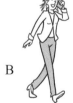 B  C

Test 2

Questions 1-5

For each question, choose the correct picture.

---

1 What's Judy wearing?

 A  B  C

2 What's Paul doing?

A B C

3 What time is the English class?

A   B   C

4 How much is the book?

A   B   C

5 When is the music lesson?

A   B   C

Day 2   独白摘要题

Test 1

Questions 6-10

For each question, write the correct answer in the gap. Write **one word** or **a number** or **a date** or **a time**.

You will hear a young man talking to a friend about his plans for tomorrow.

Manuel's Plan	
Place of meeting:	in the park
Time of the meeting:	(6) _____
Number of people coming:	(7) _____
Place to eat:	(8) _____
Distance between the music club and the park:	(9) _____-minute walk
Name of the band playing:	(10) the _____ Notes

Test 2

Questions 6-10

For each question, write the correct answer in the gap. Write **one word** or **a number** or **a date** or **a time**.

You will hear the recording of a supermarket where there are a lot of special offers.

Shop at Super Savers Stores	
Start of campaign:	Monday
Price of T-shirts:	(6) £_____
Reduction on swimwear:	(7) _____ per cent
Now at £2 a bottle:	(8) _____
Yogurts per pot:	(9) _____ pence
End of campaign:	(10) _____
Enjoy shopping at Super Savers!	

Day 3 长对话单选题

Test 1

Questions 11-15

For each question, choose the correct answer.

You will hear two friends, Emily and Alex, talking about a trip they took.

11 What was the name of the village Emily and Alex visited?

    A Green Meadow   **B** Green Valley   **C** Green Hills

12 What activity did Emily enjoy the most during their trip?

    A exploring local farms

    B meeting friendly people

    C hiking up the hills

13 What did the two girls learn about during their visit to the farm?

    A how to make traditional pies

    B how cheese is made

    C how to milk cows

14 What challenge did Emily and Alex face during their trip?

    A The local people weren't very friendly.

    B The local restaurant was closed.

    C Unexpected heavy rain.

15 What was the overall impression of Emily and Alex's trip?

    A great fun   **B** adventurous   **C** very scary

Test 2

Questions 11-15

For each question, choose the correct answer.

You will hear two friends talking about their plans for the weekend.

11 Charlie suggests they

    A go shopping.   **B** play computer games.   **C** go swimming.

12 Jason is going to a concert with

    A Charlie.   **B** his mother.   **C** his sister.

13 Charlie's favourite football team is

    A Manchester United.   **B** Chelsea.   **C** Liverpool.

14 Jason is going to the library

    A on Saturday afternoon.   **B** on Sunday afternoon.   **C** on Friday morning.

15 Jason will bring

    A some sandwiches.   **B** some cake.   **C** some pizza.

Day 4 短对话/独白单选题

Test 1

Questions 16-20

For each question, choose the correct answer.

---

16 You will hear two friends talking about school homework.

When is the deadline for History?

A on Thursday **B** on Wednesday **C** on Tuesday

17 You will hear a teacher talking to her class.

Where is the meeting point for the school trip?

A in London **B** near the park **C** outside the school's gate

18 You will hear a girl, Lisa, talking to a shop assistant.

Where is the computer she wants to buy?

A It's downstairs. **B** It's on the ground floor. **C** It's on the first floor.

19 You will hear a dad talking to his son.

What did his classmates really like?

A visiting museums **B** going to the cinema **C** going to the theatre

20 You will hear a boy, Jonah, asking for information.

Where does he buy the train tickets?

A on the Internet **B** from the ticket machines **C** at the ticket office

Test 2

Questions 16-20

For each question, choose the correct answer.

---

16 You will hear a boy, Sean, asking for information.

What time is the bus to London?

A at half past six **B** at half past four **C** at two o'clock

17 You will hear two friends talking about the weekend.

How is he going to his aunt's holiday home?

A by car　　　　　**B** by bus　　　　　**C** by train

18 You will hear a girl asking for information.

Where is the post office?

A in North Street　　　　**B** in North Road　　　　**C** in North Avenue

19 You will hear Paul and his father talking.

What does the father think about the shorts?

A Mum doesn't like shorts.

B The shorts are too expensive.

C He thinks the colours are wrong.

20 You will hear two friends talking about a birthday.

Why aren't shoes a good idea?

A Sally's grandmother doesn't like them.

B Sally bought shoes for her grandmother last year.

C Shoes can be very expensive.

Day 5　信息匹配题

Test 1

Questions 21-25

For each question, choose the correct answer.

You will hear two friends talking about a barbecue.

What is each person going to do?

Example:

0   Polly   [D]

People			Activities
21	Peter	☐	**A** clean the chairs and the tables
22	Nikki	☐	**B** bring the music
			C bake a cake
23	Emily	☐	**D** ~~do the shopping~~
24	Lucas	☐	**E** cook the food
			F cut the grass
25	Mike	☐	**G** bring ice cream
			H wash the dishes

Test 2

Questions 21-25

For each question, choose the correct answer.

You will hear two friends talking about a party.

What will each person help with?

Example:

0   Yuki   [A]

People			Help with
21	Tom	☐	**A** ~~chicken nuggets~~
22	Isabel	☐	**B** fruit juice
			C popcorn
23	Nora	☐	**D** film
24	Jason	☐	**E** music
			F balloons
25	Fred	☐	**G** photographs
			H pizza

附录 参考答案及听力原文

参考答案

Week 2

Day 2

1. interesting   2. understand   3. quiet   4. message   5. discuss   6. website

Day 3

1. castle   2. surf   3. ski   4. scary   5. crowded   6. valley

Day 4

1. look for   2. lift   3. sports kit   4. size   5. vegetables   6. wait for

Day 5

1. Hold on a moment   2. turn the volume down   3. at least

4. run out of   5. was absent from   6. save up

Weekend

I. 1. Hobbies: skateboarding, sailing, surfing, taking photos

2. Places to go: the museum, the castle, a park, the beach

3. Food: omelette, chocolate cake, dried fruit

4. Things to do at the weekend: have a picnic, go to a restaurant, have a party

II. 1. b   2. c   3. d   4. e   5. a   6. f

III. 1. A   2. C   3. A   4. A   5. B

IV. 1. C   2. C   3. B   4. B   5. A

Week 3

Day 1

I. 1. 图1 go to the party　　2. 图2 do homework　　3. 图3 ill

II. 1. 图2　　2. 图2

Day 2

I. 1. two thirty/half past two　　2. three o'clock

II. 1. 图2　　2. 图2

Day 3

I. 图1：go skateboarding　　2. 图2：ride a bike　　3. 图3：play basketball

II. 1. skateboarding　　2. play basketball

Day 4

I. 1. 这些短裤正在打折。　　2. 我要衬衫和短裤。

II. 1. A　　2. C

Day 5

I. 1. 我到达机场时，我姐姐会来接我的。　　2. 我父母那天要上班。

3. 我们计划在回家的路上去看望我们的祖父母。

II. 1. F　　2. F　　3. T

Weekend

I. 1. b　　2. a　　3. h　　4. e　　5. c　　6. d　　7. g　　8. f

II. 1. cinema　　2. guitar　　3. cash　　4. library　　5. customer　　6. storm

III. 1. station　　2. towel　　3. lunch box　　4. sailing　　5. fridge

IV. 1. B　　2. A　　3. A　　4. A　　5. C

Week 4

Day 2

I. 1. August   2. photograph   3. hundred   4. several   5. drive

II. 1. start   2. September   3. sports   4. five hundred   5. enjoyed

III. 1. T   2. F   3. T   4. F   5. T

Day 4

I. 1. Wednesday   2. remember   3. choose   4. exhibition   5. Thursday

II. 1. competition   2. take part in   3. message   4. winner   5. held

III. 1. T   2. T   3. F   4. F   5. F

Day 6

I. 1. course   2. mall   3. definitely   4. suggest   5. possibility

II. 1. know, join   2. Wednesdays, Fridays   3. half an hour   4. close to   5. interested

III. 1. F   2. T   3. T   4. F   5. F

Weekend

I.

at	in	on	无介词
half past nine the moment	February the afternoon 2024	Monday morning Fridays 20th August	last year yesterday

II. 1. eleventh   2. eleven   3. sixty   4. twelve   5. second

   6. fourth   7. September   8. twenty-six   9. November   10. Wednesday

III. 1. 8652399   2. volleyball   3. interesting   4. mother   5. soccer

IV. (1) 3/THREE   (2) CENTRAL   (3) PARTNER   (4) THURSDAY   (5) TRAIN

Week 5

Day 2

I. 1. book　　2. pity　　3. on　　4. rent　　5. full

II. 1. beginning　2. excited　3. learning about　4. fantastic　5. music festival

III. 1. F　　2. F　　3. T　　4. T　　5. F

Day 4

I. 1. practised　2. alone　3. list　4. agrees　5. band

II. 1. T　　2. F　　3. T　　4. F　　5. T

III. 1. 我以为你想加入学校乐队。

2. 如果你在下周一之前做，就不会。

3. 她太小了，不能独自旅行。

4. 我想你可以问她是否想来。

5. 还有三个名额。

Day 6

I. 1. court　2. except　3. costs　4. built　5. light

II. 1. F　　2. T　　3. F　　4. T　　5. T

III. 1. ill　2. difficult　3. small

Weekend

I. 1. famous　2. attention　3. booked　4. coach

5. journey　6. correct　7. tickets　8. packing

II. 1. C　2. G　3. F　4. E　5. A

III. 1. B　2. A　3. B　4. C　5. B

Week 6

Day 1

I. 1. pleased with　2. remember; shout at　3. bit; respect

II. 1. marks   2. hurry   3. pleased

Day 2

I. 1. exhausted; hurt   2. go straight   3. lie on

II. 1. exhausted   2. exercise   3. straight

Day 3

I. 1. 多么棒的照片啊！   2. 他们一天的课程结束了。

II. 1. running; jumping   2. ready   3. raining; indoors

Day 4

I. 1. pale   2. enough   3. stuff

II. 1. only; school stuff   2. lend

Day 5

I. 1. looked out of   2. weather; temperature; higher   3. umbrella; starting

II. 1. mean   2. high   3. forecast

Weekend

I. 1. information   2. discount   3. storm   4. bored   5. foggy   6. stadium

II. 1. A   2. C   3. B   4. A   5. B

III. 1. C   2. F   3. E   4. D   5. B

IV. 1. B   2. C   3. A   4. B   5. B

Week 7

Day 2

I. 1. oranges; grapes   2. hungry   3. chose; because   4. bringing   5. telephoned; bowl

II. 1. nearly   2. ready   3. cook   4. choose   5. popular

III. 1. F   2. T   3. F   4. F   5. T

Day 4

I. 1. market 　 2. sports centre 　 3. restaurant 　 4. museum 　 5. bookshop

II. 1. enjoyed 　 2. decide 　 3. walking 　 4. sitting 　 5. drew; selling

III. 1. T 　 2. F 　 3. T 　 4. F

Day 6

I. 1. artist 　 2. dentist 　 3. pilot 　 4. mechanic 　 5. actor

II. 1. paintings 　 2. travel around 　 3. hospital 　 4. articles 　 5. machines

III. 1. T 　 2. F 　 3. T 　 4. T 　 5. F

Weekend

I. 1. cheese 　 2. salad 　 3. bring 　 4. email 　 5. decide

　 6. repair 　 7. build 　 8. enjoy

II. 1. A 　 2. C 　 3. B 　 4. B 　 5. A

III. 1. F 　 2. T 　 3. F 　 4. F 　 5. T 　 6. T 　 7. T 　 8. T

IV. 1. E 　 2. D 　 3. A 　 4. B 　 5. H

听力原文—练习部分

Week 2

Weekend

III. 1. That student has trouble using chopsticks.

2. Lee's birthday party starts at fifteen to nine in a hotel this evening.

3. The box is very heavy, and you must use both hands to carry it.

4. A: What's the weather like today?

B: It is sunny. But the radio says it will be rainy tomorrow.

5. Girl: Do you ride a bike home?

Boy: Yes, sometimes. I'd like to take a bus most of the time. It takes less time.

IV.

1. W: Peter, did you visit your grandparents last Saturday?

   M: No, I visited them last Sunday morning.

2. W: Are you OK?You look very tired.

   M: I couldn't sleep well last night. The workers were building a tall building in my block

   day and night. It's so noisy!

3. W: Oh no!

   M: What happened?

   W: I lost my wallet! I remembered I put it into my bag. But now it isn't there.

4. M: What can l do for you, Ms.Zhang?

   W: I want to buy a ticket to New York on October thirtieth.

5. M: Those are very nice shirts. How much are they?

   W: Five dollars each or two for nine dollars. They are on sale today.

   M: I'll take this yellow one.

Week 3

Day 1

II. 1. I have to study at home to prepare the exam.

2. I was ill, so I stayed at home to have a rest.

Day 2

II. 1. The plane will take off at half past three.

2. A: When does the party start?

   B: The party starts at half past two.

Day 3

II. 1. He sometimes goes skateboarding on weekends.

2. Why don't we play basketball this afternoon?

Day 4

II.

M: Excuse me, are these shorts in the sale?

F: Yes, sir. Everything on that shelf is five pounds.

M: I'll take this shirt too.

F: That's fifteen pounds, so with the shorts that will be twenty pounds.

M: Great, I'll take them.

Day 5

II.

F: Will someone meet you when you arrive at the airport, Peter?

M: Yes. My parents will be at work, but my older sister will. She's just passed her driving test!

F: That's good news.

M: And my grandfather lives near the airport so we're going to visit him on the way home.

F: That's nice.

Weekend

IV.

1. M: How do you usually go to school, Jenny?

   W: I used to go by bus. And now I am used to riding my bike to school.

2. W: It's a quarter past eight. You are ten minutes late for the first class. What happened to you, Tom?

   M: Sorry, there was a lot of traffic on the way.

3. M: Linda, you didn't come to school yesterday. What was the matter?

   W: I'm sorry. I was sick in bed. My parents were busy and didn't take me to the hospital.

4. W: Do you have any rules at home, Bob?

   M: Yes, I can watch TV or play computer games on weekends' nights. But I can read some books after l finish my homework.

5. W: I want to have a picnic next Sunday. What will the weather be like?

   M: Though it is raining now, the radio says it will be fine next Sunday. I think we can go for a picnic.

Week 4

Day 2

II.

1. The camps start on the fifteenth of June.

2. Most students then spend September travelling around and having a holiday before they come home.

3. You must be good at sports or languages.

4. You could save over five hundred pounds during your time there.

5. Several students from this college went to work for Sunshine Holidays last year and enjoyed it.

III.

F: Several students from this college went to work for Sunshine Holidays last year and enjoyed it. So I'm going to give you some information about working in their summer camps this year.

The camps start on the fifteenth of June so you must be free from then until August the twentieth. Most students then spend September travelling around and having a holiday before they come home.

The camps are for children who are between ten and fifteen years old and to work there you have to be nineteen. So that's OK for most of you.

You don't need to be good at sports or languages but they only want people who can drive. That's because you'll take the children out on trips by car.

Each week you'll get sixty-five pounds, so you could save over five hundred pounds during your time there.

If you're interested, you need to write a letter and send it with a photo to Sunshine Holidays. So, does anyone have any questions…?

Day 4

II.

1. I'm going to give you some information about this year's short-film-making competition.

2. The students who want to take part in the competition must send two short films.

3. The winners will receive an email message before the competition day.

4. The winner of this year's competition will get a backpack.

5. The short film exhibition will be held on the third floor of the school.

III.

F: Hello everybody. I'm going to give you some information about this year's short-film-making competition. As you may remember, know, last year's films are about plants; but this year, students have to make a short film focused on animals. You can choose to make a film of cats or dogs and send it to the school office from August 15th to August 20th. The competition will be on the last Wednesday of August.

The students who want to take part in the competition must send two short films, but only one will be chosen for the competition. The winners will receive an email message before the competition day. There will be three prizes: the third prize is a T-shirt; the second prize is a cup and the winner of this year's competition will get a backpack.

Lastly, remember to tell your family and friends that the short film exhibition will be held on the third floor of the school. Now, if you have any questions, I'll be happy to answer all of them.

Day 6

II.

1. As you know, you all have the possibility to join Mrs Halliday's guitar lessons

2. Lessons are on Wednesdays and Fridays.

3. A single lesson for three students is 35 pounds an hour or £20 for half an hour.

4. You must go to Mrs Halliday's house which is very close to Queen Shopping Mall.

5. If you're interested in learning to play guitar, please give her a call.

III.

F: Good morning, boys and girls. As you know, you all have the possibility to join Mrs

Halliday's guitar lessons, starting from next month. That's H-A-double L-I-D-A-Y.

Lessons are on Wednesdays and Fridays, but on Wednesdays you already have the Spanish course with Mr Sheldon, so your day will definitely be Friday.

Now, the price. A single lesson for three students is 35 pounds an hour or £20 for half an hour. I suggest you start with the one-hour lesson, then once you know the basics you can do half an hour.

You must go to Mrs Halliday's house which is very close to Queen Shopping Mall. The exact address is 205 Main Street. If you're interested in learning to play guitar, please give her a call. Her number is 0865 945371. Did you get it right? I'll say it again: 0865 945371. The best time to call her is between seven and nine. Is that clear to everyone?

Weekend

III. Hi! My name is Anna. I'm from the UK. My telephone number is eight six five two three double nine. I like to play volleyball. I play it at school with my friends. I can play it well now. My brother Dave can't play volleyball, but he can play ping-pong. He thinks it's interesting and easy. Sally is my mother. She likes watching TV. And she thinks it is very relaxing. My father Jimmy doesn't like watching TV. He likes sports. He is good at soccer. He says it's really interesting.

IV. I'm going to go somewhere very exciting next week. Yes, you're right. That's London. There's a lot to do in London. I''m going to visit three museums. I'll stay in a lovely hotel in the central part of the city. It's called the Grange Hotel. I've already booked a room. I don't like traveling alone, so I'm going to go with my business partner. We have the same interests. I'm going to be there from Saturday to Thursday, so I'll stay in London for six days. Many people like to drive to London. They think it's convenient and they can go anywhere they like. But I like to go there by train. Hopefully, I will have a wonderful journey.

Week 5

Day 2

II.

1. Are you free at the beginning of next month?

2. Are you excited about the trip?

3. I really enjoyed learning about their history.

4. When I'm in Dublin I always have lots of fish—it's fantastic.

5. It's a pity the music festival won't be on.

III.

M: Hi, Laura. Some of us are going for a weekend in Dublin this year. Are you free at the beginning of next month?

F: Yes, I'd love to come.

M: Great!

F: Who else is going?

M: I asked my cousins, but they're playing in a tennis competition—so there'll be four of us from my office, and you.

F: Where are we staying?

M: I tried to book a guest-house. It was full, but visitors can rent rooms in the university during the holidays. We'll do that—it's cheaper than a hotel.

F: Excellent. Are you taking your new camera?

M: Yes, some maps of the city too. But you'll need a coat! It often rains.

F: OK!

M: Have you been before?

F: Yes! The centre's busy—the shops are always full of people! My friends and I loved all the beautiful buildings—I really enjoyed learning about their history.

M: Yeah!

F: So, are you excited about the trip?

M: Yeah but it's a pity the music festival won't be on. When I'm in Dublin I always have lots of fish—it's fantastic. There's a new art exhibition—you might like it, but I'm not interested.

F: Yeah, maybe!

Day 4

II.

F: Hello, Louis. I see your name isn't on the list for the after-school music club.

M: Yes, I know that, Miss Martha.

F: I thought you wanted to be in the school band.

M: I do. I've been thinking about joining, but I'm not sure if I am good enough.

F: If you practise regularly, yes.

M: That's the problem. I can't come three times a week.

F: Is there too much homework?

M: No, the homework is fine with me. I have to go home with my little sister. My parents both work, so they can't pick her up after school. And she's too young to travel alone.

F: I see. Is she interested in music?

M: Not as much as studying.

F: Do you think she might join the music club? Then you could still go home together.

M: That's a good idea. I think she might agree to come and watch but she won't take part.

F: OK. Then I think you could ask her if she wants to come.

M: Sure. So, it's not too late to add my name to the list?

F: Not if you do it before next Monday. There are still three places left.

M: OK.

Day 6

II.

M: Hello, Sue. Have you been to the new sports centre yet?

F: No, Tony, where is it?

M: In Queen Street. You know, near Peace Square, behind the Molly Shopping Mall.

F: Oh. Is it good?

M: Yes, it's big and light! You can do a lot of sports. I played badminton and basketball last weekend.

F: What about tennis?

M: They haven't built the tennis courts yet, but they are planning to build one next year.

F: Is it expensive?

M: Not really, Sue. It costs £120 per year if you're 14 to 18, and £80 if you're under 14.

F: Oh, that's great, because I'm still 13.

M: Also, it stays open late until 10 o'clock on Monday, Wednesday, and Friday.

F: Oh, great. How did you get there?

M: I took the number 18 bus. It's only 15 minutes from the bus station. Don't get bus 16 because you have to walk a long way. Would you like to go next week?

F: Sure. Any day except Tuesday.

M: Well, why don't we go on Wednesday? Then we can stay late.

F: Yes, OK. Let's meet after school.

Weekend

III. Now be quiet, boys and girls! In order to improve your spoken English, an English Speech Competition will be held in our school hall. It is from 3 p.m. to 5 p.m. on September 12th. If you want to take part in this competition, go to your English teacher Mrs. Jill's office to enter your name before July 20th. You will give a speech on how to learn English well. The winners can go to an English summer camp for free. I hope everyone will take part in it.

Week 6

Day 1

I. 1. I'm very pleased with your work.

2. You really must remember that other classes in rooms near us can't do their work if you shout at one another.

3. Let's all show a bit more respect for other people.

Day 2

I. 1. Everyone did really well today but I'm exhausted now and my legs really hurt.

2. I'm going to go straight home and ask mum if I can have a pizza for dinner.

3. I'm going to lie on my bed and listen to music all evening.

Day 3

II. 1. They were all moving around so quickly—running and jumping about.

2. The little ones were all ready to go home.

3. It was raining, but they just wanted to run around after being indoors for so many hours.

Day 4

II. 1. This was the only one in the shop that was big enough for all my school stuff.

2. Mum had to lend me some money.

Day 5

I. 1. Have you looked out of the window this morning?

2. The weather forecast says the temperature's definitely going to be higher than yesterday.

3. Take an umbrella because it's just starting to rain.

Weekend

IV.

1. You'll hear the son and mother talking about what to drink. What does the boy decide to drink at last?

   F: I'd like another cup of coffee, Dad.

   M: Well, you have had too much coffee. It will make you too excited to sleep at night. What about some juice?

   F: I don't like it. Please give me a glass of yogurt.

2. You'll hear two friends talking about the weekend plan. What will Lisa do this weekend?

   M: Hello, Lisa. Shall we have a picnic this Sunday?

   F: I'm afraid I can't. I will have an English test next week. I'm not ready for it now.

3. You'll hear a man and a shop assistant talking about the clothes price. How much should the man pay?

   M: Those are very nice shirts. How much are they?

   W: Five dollars each or two for nine dollars. They are on sale today.

   M: I'll take this yellow one.

4. You'll hear a man and a woman talking together. Where are they?

   M: What's wrong with your son, Madam?

   F: He has the flu and doesn't want to eat anything.

   M: How long has he been like this?

   F: Since yesterday morning.

   M: Let me have a look. Oh, never mind. There's nothing serious. He'd better take some medicine and drink some hot water.

5. You will hear a woman talking on the phone. Why's she upset?

   F: I feel so upset! I can't see it anywhere. It probably fell out of my bag on the way to the station. I can't buy a ticket now! I'm going back to work to ask if anybody has seen it, or can lend me some money. I have an appointment for an eye test this afternoon—I'll be late now!

Week 7

Day 2

I. 1. Barbara's going to bring some oranges and grapes.

   2. Everyone gets hungry at parties, don't they?

   3. I chose chicken because it's more popular than fish.

   4. What's Michael bringing—he's coming, isn't he?

   5. I telephoned him and he's going to make a big bowl of sliced tomatoes and onions.

III.

   M: Are you nearly ready for your birthday party on Saturday, Maria?

   F: I think so, Simon. I've made a cake and my friends are bringing the other food.

   M: That's a good idea.

   F: Barbara's going to bring some oranges and grapes.

   M: And I'll bring some bread and cheese from the market if you like. Everyone gets hungry at parties, don't they?

   F: Thanks, Simon. But you don't need to bring bread because Anita's bringing that. She wanted to bring ice cream but I think the weather's too cold!

   M: Mm, it is. Perhaps Peter can help. He likes cooking, doesn't he?

F: Yes, he emailed me and asked me to choose roast chicken or fish. I chose chicken because it's more popular than fish. What do you think?

M: That sounds great! What's Michael bringing—he's coming, isn't he?

F: Yes, he loves parties! I telephoned him and he's going to make a big bowl of sliced tomatoes and onions.

M: Lovely!

Day 4

II. 1. The art class this week was really interesting, Ann. I really enjoyed it.

2. I couldn't decide between the museum and the market.

3. We were walking to the market together.

4. I saw her in Main Street sitting at a table having a sandwich.

5. At last I drew a picture of people selling fruit and vegetables.

III.

M: The art class this week was really interesting, Ann. I really enjoyed it.

F: So did I, Paul. I liked drawing different places or buildings of this city. Is this your picture of the park?

M: Yes. What did you draw?

F: I couldn't decide between the museum and the market. At last I drew a picture of people selling fruit and vegetables. Do you know what Andrew drew?

M: Yes, I met him in a bookshop after the lesson. His picture was of some people in the cafe reading books.

F: I know Grace loves drawing water. Did she go to the sea?

M: Well, she went to the sports centre and drew some people swimming. What did Colin draw? You know, he is the best artist.

F: We were walking to the market together but then he saw someone buying clothes in a shop and he stopped to draw that. What about Marina?

M: I saw her in Main Street sitting at a table having a sandwich. She was drawing a waitress talking to a lady.

F: What an interesting art lesson!

Day 6

II. 1. I love paintings and drawings.

2. He loves flying, so he'd like to fly planes and travel around the world.

3. She wanted to be a teacher but now she wants to work at the hospital.

4. She wants to write stories or articles for newspapers.

5. He wants to design and build machines in the future.

III.

M: Suzie, we talked about future jobs in school today, which was really interesting.

 F: So Eason, what do you want to do?

M: I love paintings and drawings. So I want to be an artist.

 F: Sound great! What is David's dream job?

M: He loves flying, so he'd like to fly planes and travel around the world.

 F: Oh, really! Amazing! Then let me guess, Tanya wants to be a teacher, doesn't she?

M: She wanted to be a teacher but now she wants to work at the hospital. You know her father is a doctor there, and she wants to help people with their teeth.

 F: That sounds like a good job too. And Julie?

M: She likes reading and writing, so she wants to write stories or articles for newspapers.

 F: She'll be good at that. What about Eric?

M: He's always helping his dad repair cars at the weekend. So that's what he wants to do.

 F: Cool! Does Ricky know what he wants to do?

M: Oh, handsome Ricky! He acted well in the school play. But he wants to design and build machines in the future.

 F: Wow! That's impressive.

Weekend

IV.

M: Hi, Amy, did you have a good time at your birthday party?

 F: Yes. I had so much fun. I received many amazing birthday presents. I got this from my mum. Now I can put all the pictures I have taken with my camera in it.

M: That's great! What did your dad get you? Did he buy you a new mobile phone?

F: Actually, I got a mobile phone from my grandpa. And my dad bought me a keyboard. He knew I had problem typing on my computer.

M: What about your brother? Did he get you another T-shirt this year?

F: No, he gave me this sweater I am wearing. It's nice, right?

M: Of course! You look really beautiful on this. What did your grandma get you?

F: My hands get cold easily in winter. So she gave me these to keep my hands warm.

M: They're lovely!

Week 8

Day 1

Test 1

1. B   2. C   3. A   4. A   5. A

[答案详解]

1. 本题考查新的西班牙语老师的名字。根据对话中的 "the one who teaches Spanish" 得知，接下来要谈论的就是西班牙语老师，下一句回复说到 "it can be Angela"，所以正确答案为Angela，故选B。选项C的Andrea是对话者的名字；选项A的Agatha是法语老师的名字。

[听力原文]

What's the name of the new Spanish teacher?

A: Hi! Andrea. I've just met the new teacher.

B: Do you mean Agatha, the French teacher?

A: No, the one who teaches Spanish.

B: Oh, it can be Angela then. You probably met her.

2. 本题考查要做的事情。根据Josh提到的 "I'm going to sleep all day." 可知，他打算一整天都睡觉，故正确答案为C。选项B是 "go swimming"，是另一个对话者提出的建议，但是被Josh否了。选项A是 "go skiing"，另一个对话者描述时说 "we can't go skiing." 所以也可排除。

[听力原文]

What is Josh doing tomorrow?

A: Hi Josh, why don't we go swimming tomorrow?

B: Tomorrow? I'm not sure I can.

A: Why not? There's a storm outside, we can't go skiing.

B: I know, that's why I'm going to sleep all day.

A: Oh Josh, shame on you!

3. 本题考查香蕉的价格。对话中提到"Bananas are cheaper too, they're two pounds thirty. （香蕉也便宜，是2.30镑。）"。故A为正确答案。选项B是苹果的价格；选项C是草莓的价格。

[听力原文]

How much are the bananas?

A: Hello. How much are the strawberries?

B: They're three pounds twenty.

A: Oh. Is there anything cheaper?

B: Apples are one pound eighty. Bananas are cheaper too, they're two pounds thirty.

A: I'll have the apples then, thanks.

4. 本题考查生日时间。对话中两人在商量去看电影的时间，Robbie说到"My mum's birthday's on Tuesday. （我妈妈的生日是在星期二。）"，所以A为正确答案。选项B的"Thursday"是另外一个对话者的生日。选项C的Friday是Robbie的奶奶的生日。

[听力原文]

When's Robbie's mum's birthday?

A: Hi Robbie, shall we go to the cinema on Friday?

B: I'm afraid I can't, it's my grandma's birthday.

A: What about on Tuesday, then?

B: My mum's birthday's on Tuesday, why don't we go on Thursday?

A: I can't, it's my birthday on Thursday!

5. 本题考查食物。对话中服务员说到"We've got fried eggs and chips here on the menu. （菜单上有煎蛋和炸薯条。）"。男孩也回复说"I'll have that. （我要这些。）"。所以男

孩点的食物是"煎蛋和炸薯条"，故正确答案为A。

[听力原文]

What does the boy order?

A: I'd like a hamburger with chips, please.

B: I'm afraid we haven't got hamburgers today. How about some fish?

A: No, I don't like fish. Have you got any cheese, or eggs?

B: <u>We've got fried eggs and chips here on the menu.</u>

A: <u>I'll have that.</u> And a cola, please.

Test 2

1. A   2. C   3. B   4. C   5. C

[答案详解]

1. 本题考查人物描述。根据对话中的"Judy is the girl over there, she's wearing white trousers and a jacket."可知，Judy穿着白色长裤和夹克，故本题选A。

[听力原文]

What's Judy wearing?

A: Lisa, do you know the name of that girl?

B: Which one? The one with the white skirt is Emma.

A: No, not that one. I'm talking about the girl with the white jacket. Isn't her name Judy?

B: Oh that one. No, she's called Janet. <u>Judy is the girl over there, she's wearing white trousers and a jacket.</u>

A: Oh yes, there she is.

2. 本题考查某人正在做的事情。对话中提到三件事情："do homework（做作业）"，"play video games（玩电子游戏）"，"watch a film on his tablet（在平板电脑上看电影）"。提到"do homework"时，对话者说"He's already done it with Jack.（他已经和杰克做完了。）"，提到"watch a film"时，对话者说"The tablet's in the kitchen.（平板电脑在厨房里。）"。因此这两项都可以排除。根据对话中的"I'm sure he's playing video games."可知，Paul在玩电子游戏，故选C。

[听力原文]

What's Paul doing?

A: Where's Paul?

B: I think he's upstairs.

A: Is he doing his homework?

B: No, he's already done it with Jack. I'm sure he's playing video games.

A: Isn't he watching a film on his tablet?

B: No, the tablet's in the kitchen.

3. 本题考查英语课程时间。根据对话中提到的 "I've just met Sarah and Stephen and they told me it's at ten fifteen in room 13." 可知，课程将于十点十五分在13号房间开始，故选项B为正确答案。

[听力原文]

What time is the English class?

A: Hurry up, the lesson starts in five minutes.

B: No, it doesn't. It starts at ten fifteen.

A: Are you sure? I read on the website that it's at five past ten in Room 15.

B: I don't think so. I've just met Sarah and Stephen and they told me it's at ten fifteen in room 13.

A: OK then. I'll see you there.

4. 本题考查图书的价格。根据对话中提到的 "It was fifteen pounds fifty, but with the discount I only paid four pounds sixty." 可知，这本书本来是15.50英镑，但是由于有折扣，所以只付了4.60英镑，故本题选C。

[听力原文]

How much is the book?

A: I've just been to the new bookshop in town. Their collection of fantasy novels is incredible!

B: I don't like fantasy, I prefer historical novels.

A: Then you really must go! You'll find a lot of historical novels at a very low price, I've just bought this book about the French Revolution.

B: Interesting. <u>How much did you pay for it?</u>

A: <u>It was fifteen pounds fifty, but with the discount I only paid four pounds sixty.</u>

B: Wow! I think I'll go now!

5. 本题考查音乐课的时间。对话中两人在商量去看电影的时间。当提到"Thursday"时，Nick说"I've got a music lesson at 7."。由此得知，音乐课是在星期四，故本题选C。

[听力原文]

When is the music lesson?

A: What are you doing on Tuesday, Nick?

B: I'm going to a concert with my music teacher. Why?

A: I'd like to see the new film at the Olympia Cinema. Would you like to come?

B: Yes, but I'm pretty busy this week. I am free on Wednesday.

A: I can't on Wednesday, I'm going to visit my grandma. <u>What about Thursday?</u>

B: <u>I've got a music lesson at 7.</u> Let's go on Friday after dinner.

A: Yes, good idea.

Day 2

Test 1

6. 7/SEVEN   7. 8/EIGHT   8. CAFE   9. TEN   10. BLUE

[答案详解]

6. 本题考查会面时间。根据录音中的"so we're meeting in the park at the small cafe next to the lake at seven"可知，相约见面的时间是七点钟，故本空填入SEVEN。

7. 本题考查人数。根据录音中的"There are going to be eight people."可知，将会有8个人，故本空填入EIGHT。

8. 本题考查用餐地点。根据录音中的"The cafe has some nice food, so we can eat there and watch the sunset over the lake.（咖啡馆有一些不错的食物，所以我们可以在那里吃饭，在湖面上看日落。）"可知，他们将要在咖啡馆用餐，故本空填入CAFE。

9. 本题考查步行时长。根据录音中的"After that, we're going to a music club. It is only a ten-minute walk from the park.（之后，我们要去一个音乐俱乐部。离公园只有十分钟的步行路程。）"可知，从公园步行10分钟就到音乐俱乐部了，故本空填入TEN。

10. 本题考查乐队名称。根据录音中的 "Our favourite band, the Blue Notes, are playing.（我们最喜欢的乐队，蓝调乐队正在演奏。）" 可知，演奏的乐队是 "the Blue Notes"，故本空填入BLUE。

[听力原文]

You will hear a young man talking to a friend about his plans for tomorrow.

Man: Hi Lucas, this is Manuel. I want to tell you about what we're doing tomorrow–that's Tuesday. It's David's birthday and we're organizing a surprise party. So, we're meeting in the park at six thirty. No, sorry. Jane can't come as early as that because she's got football training, (6) so we're meeting in the park at the small cafe next to the lake at seven.

(7) There are going to be eight people. Can you get a table for eight? Thanks. (8) The cafe has some nice food, so we can eat there and watch the sunset over the lake. You can find their telephone number online.

(9) After that, we're going to a music club. It is only a ten-minute walk from the park.

(10) Our favourite band, the Blue Notes, are playing. It's their only date in town. The concert starts at 9 p.m. and finishes at 10.30 p.m., just in time for the last bus home. See you tomorrow.

Test 2

6. 5/FIVE   7. 30/THIRTY   8. JUICES   9. 50/FIFTY   10. FRIDAY

[答案详解]

6. 本题考查价格。根据录音中的 "T-shirts are three pounds cheaper and now cost only five pounds.（T恤衫便宜了3英镑，现在只花了5英镑。）" 可知，T恤衫现在的价格是5英镑，故本空填入5/FIVE。

7. 本题考查数字。根据录音中的 "All swimwear is now thirty percent less than last week.（现在所有的泳装都比上周少了30%。）" 可知，泳装降价了30%，故本空填入30/THIRTY。

8. 本题考查物品。根据录音中的 "Our juices are now only two pounds a bottle.（我们的果汁现在一瓶只有2英镑。）" 可知，现在一瓶2英镑的价格可以买到果汁，故本空填入JUICES。

9. 本题考查价格。根据录音中的 "Yogurts are just fifty pence a pot." 可知，一壶酸奶只要50便士，故本空填入50/FIFTY。

10. 本题考查时间。录音中提到 "These great offers end on Friday.（这些优惠将于周五结束。）"，题干中的 "campaign" 指的就是这场促销活动，故本空填入FRIDAY。

[听力原文]

You will hear the recording of a supermarket where there are a lot of special offers.

Man: Thank you for calling Super Savers Stores. We now have low prices in store. The sales campaign starts on Monday 21st. Don't miss the opportunity to buy a lot and spend very little!

All school items, except school books and backpacks, are now ten percent less. Notebooks are all one pound. Don't forget to visit the graphic novels section for the best offers.

You can also save money in our clothes department. (6) T-shirts are three pounds cheaper and now cost only five pounds. (7) All swimwear is now thirty percent less than last week. Our beautiful bikinis are only twenty-two pounds fifty.

Finally, you must pay a visit to the food and drink department. All the snacks you can eat for one pound twenty! (8) Our juices are now only two pounds a bottle and (9) yogurts are just fifty pence a pot. Buy! Buy! Don't forget: (10) these great offers end on Friday.

Day 3

Test 1

11. B   12. C   13. B   14. C   15. B

[答案详解]

11. 根据对话中的 "We decided to visit a small village in the hills called Green Valley.（我们决定参观山上一个叫Green Valley的小村庄。）" 可知，Emily和Alex去的地方的名字叫 "Green Valley"。故选B。

12. 对话中主持人提问 "What did you enjoy the most about your visit?（你这次旅行最喜欢什么？）"，Emily回复说 "I absolutely adored when we went hiking.（当我们去徒步旅行

时，我非常喜欢。）"。由此可知，Emily最喜欢"hiking"，故选C。

13. 根据对话中的"We went to a nearby farm and learned how they make cheese.（我们去了附近的一个农场，学习了如何制作奶酪。）"可知，她们学习了如何制作奶酪，故选B。

14. 根据对话中的"We read online about fine weather, but it had heavy rain showers in the end.（我们在网上看到天气很好，但最后还是下了大雨。）"可知，她们在旅途中面临的挑战是"unexpected heavy rain"，即"突如其来的大雨"，故选C。

15. 根据对话中的"It sounds like an adventurous and memorable trip.（这听起来像是一次冒险和难忘的旅行。）"可知，对于她们旅行的"overall impression（整体印象）"是冒险的和难忘的，故选B。

[听力原文]

You will hear two friends, Emily and Alex, talking about a trip they took.

Host: Good morning, listeners! Today on our show, we have Emily and Alex joining us to talk about their recent trip to the countryside. Hi, Emily and Alex!

Emily: Hi there!

Alex: Hello!

Host: So, tell us about your trip. Where did you go?

Emily: (11) We decided to visit a small village in the hills called Green Valley.

Alex: Yes, it was a beautiful place with amazing landscapes and friendly people.

Host: Sounds wonderful! What did you enjoy the most about your visit?

Emily: (12) I absolutely adored when we went hiking. We explored different paths and enjoyed the most beautiful views of the countryside.

Alex: Absolutely! We also saw a waterfall during one of our hikes. It was fantastic.

Host: Did you try any local food while you were there?

Emily: Oh, yes! We had a chance to taste some traditional dishes at a typical restaurant. The homemade pies were delicious!

Alex: And don't forget about the farm visit! (13) We went to a nearby farm and learned how they make cheese. It was a fun and educational experience.

Host: That sounds like a lot of fun! Were there any challenges during your trip?

Emily: Well, the weather was changeable. (14) We read online about fine weather, but it had heavy rain showers in the end.

Alex: Also, we met a lot of cows on our way to the top of a hill and they didn't want to move.

Emily: Oh yes! We didn't know what to do but then a local woman arrived and helped us. It was a bit scary but fun as well.

Host: (15) It sounds like an adventurous and memorable trip. Thank you, Emily and Alex, for sharing your experience with us!

Alex: Thank you for having us!

Test 2

11. B   12. C   13. A   14. A   15. C

[答案详解]

11. 根据对话中的 "What about playing some computer games or watching a film?（玩电脑游戏或看电影怎么样？）" 可知，Charlie建议两人玩电脑游戏或看电影，结合选项，故选B。

12. 根据对话中的 "I'm going to a pop concert with my sister.（我要和我姐姐一起去听一场流行音乐会。）" 可知，Jason要和姐姐一起去听音乐会，故选C。

13. 根据对话中的 "Go Manchester United, go!!（加油，曼联，加油！）" 可知，Charlie最喜欢的足球队是曼联，故选A。

14. 对话中Charlie问Jason "Are you free on Saturday in the morning?（你星期六早上有空吗？）"，Jason回答说上午要去看望aunt，接着又说 "Then I'm going to the library in the afternoon.（然后我下午去图书馆。）"。由此可知，Jason会在星期六下午去图书馆，故选A。

15. 根据对话中的 "I'll bring some pizza.（我会带一些比萨来。）" 可知，Jason会带一些比萨去Charlie家，故选C。

[听力原文]

You will hear two friends talking about their plans for the weekend.

Charlie: Hey Jason, do you want to meet up this weekend and do something?

Jason: Great idea, what do you want to do?

Charlie: (11) <u>What about playing some computer games or watching a film?</u>

Jason: I don't want to watch a film, but we could play some computer games. Actually, we can't meet on Saturday evening. (12) <u>I'm going to a pop concert with my sister.</u>

Charlie: I'm busy too, on Saturday evening, I'm going to a football match. My favourite football team is playing against Chelsea. (13) <u>Go Manchester United, go!!</u> Last week they beat Liverpool. I'll be home late. (14) <u>Are you free on Saturday in the morning?</u>

Jason: No, I'm sorry. I'm going to my aunt Molly first of all. She is making my favourite cake. (14) <u>Then I'm going to the library in the afternoon.</u> I need some more books to read.

Charlie: What about Sunday then?

Jason: I promised to help my dad with the gardening in the afternoon. But maybe after five o'clock?

Charlie: Sounds good. Do you want to come to my house? My parents won't be home. They're going out for dinner.

Jason: Yeah, sure. Sounds good! (15) <u>I'll bring some pizza.</u>

Charlie: Brilliant. See you on Sunday then.

Day 4

Test 1

16. A   17. C   18. C   19. A   20. A

[答案详解]

16. 根据对话中提到的 "I think the deadline for history is on Thursday.（我认为历史的截止日期是星期四。）" 可知，答案为A。

[听力原文]

You will hear two friends talking about school homework. When is the deadline for history?

A: When have we got to give our homework to the teacher?

B: <u>I think the deadline for history is on Thursday</u> and spanish is on Friday.

A: What about maths? Isn't that on Thursday?

B: Umm – you're right. So, history must be the day before that.

A: Today's Tuesday – we only have a day left to do it!

17. 根据对话中提到的 "We're going by coach, so all students need to be outside the main gate at seven o'clock.（我们乘长途汽车去，所以所有的学生都需要在七点钟到大门外。）" 可知，学校旅行的集合地点是学校大门外，故选C。

[听力原文]

You will hear a teacher talking to her class. Where is the meeting point for the school trip?

A: Don't forget that we're going on our trip to London tomorrow.

B: Do we have to come to the classroom before we go?

A: No, you don't. We're going by coach, so all students need to be outside the main gate at seven o'clock.

B: That's very early for me, I live near the park, it's very far from school.

A: Can't you ask your parents to drive you to school before 7?

B: I'll ask my mum. Thanks.

18. 根据对话中提到的 "You can find some at a very good price on the first floor on the left, near the smartphones.（你可以在一楼左边的智能手机附近找到一些价格优惠的。）" 可知，Lisa可以在一楼买到想要的电脑，故选C。

[听力原文]

You will hear a girl, Lisa, talking to a shop assistant. Where is the computer she wants to buy?

A: Excuse me, I'm looking for a new computer.

B: OK. You can see all our computers downstairs.

A: I went downstairs but I only saw new and very expensive ones. Where are the special offers? They aren't here on the ground floor.

B: You can find some at a very good price on the first floor on the left, near the smartphones.

A: Is there someone who can help me to choose the best one?

B: Of course. Just ask a member of our staff.

19. 根据对话开头可知他们谈论的是去参观博物馆的情况，后面又提到 "Most of my classmates really enjoyed looking at things from the past but not me.（我的大多数同学都很喜欢看过去的事情，但我不喜欢。）" 由此可知，"things from the past" 指的就是博物馆里的东西，所以他的同学们都很喜欢去博物馆，故选A。

[听力原文]

You will hear a dad talking to his son. What did his classmates really like?

A: How was your school trip to the museum?

B: Well, the place was very full. It was difficult to see anything.

A: Oh. I'm sorry you didn't have a good time.

B: Most of my classmates really enjoyed looking at things from the past but not me.

A: What do you like?

B: I prefer going to the cinema. It's much more exciting.

A: Well I don't think your teachers will take you to the cinema. What about the theatre?

B: I like the theatre, but my classmates say it's boring.

20.对话中男孩在购买火车票，对方建议 "Why don't you buy them online?（你为什么不在 网上购买呢？）"，男孩回复说 "That's a good idea.（好主意。）"。由此可知，男孩 会在网上买票，故选A。

[听力原文]

You will hear a boy, Jonah, asking for information. Where does he buy the train tickets?

A: Excuse me. Could you tell me where I can buy the train tickets?

B: Do you want to travel today?

A: No. I want to go next week.

B: You can get them at the ticket machines, but only one is working today. Have you tried the ticket office?

A: Yes, but there are a lot of people.

B: Why don't you buy them online?

A: That's a good idea, thank you very much.

Test 2

16. A   17. A   18. A   19. C   20. C

[答案详解]

16.对话中男孩在询问去伦敦的公交车时间，工作人员回复说 "I think it's at half past six. （我认为是六点半）"，由此可知，正确答案为A。

[听力原文]

You will hear a boy, Sean, asking for information. What time is the bus to London?

A: Excuse me. Do you know what time the next bus goes to London?

B: I think it's at half past six.

A: Oh no! It's only half past four now. That's another two hours to wait.

B: Let me look at the timetable again. I'm sorry but that is the correct time.

17. 根据对话中提到的 "My aunt's taking me in her new car!（我姑姑要用她的新车载我去！）" 可知，他会乘坐小汽车去他姑姑的度假屋，故选A。

[听力原文]

You will hear two friends talking about the weekend. How is he going to his aunt's holiday home?

A: What are you doing this weekend?

B: I'm going to visit my aunt in her holiday home.

A: Does it take a long time to get there?

B: It can! The bus takes a really long time.

A: What about the train?

B: I'm not going by train! My aunt's taking me in her new car!

18. 根据对话中提到的 "It's at the end of North Street opposite the post office.（它在北街尽头，邮局对面。）" 可知，邮局也在北街，故选A。

[听力原文]

You will hear a girl asking for information. Where is the post office?

A: Excuse me. I'm looking for a bookshop in North Road.

B: There isn't a bookshop in North Road. Do you mean North Street?

A: Oh, I'm not sure. On the map there's North Road, North Avenue and North Street.

B: I know. Look. Go down North Road and then turn left into North Street.

A: Where exactly is the bookshop?

B: It's at the end of North Street opposite the post office.

19. 对话中父子两人在为妈妈挑选短裤，爸爸提到 "Your mum doesn't really like those

colours.（你妈妈真的不喜欢那些颜色）"。由此可知，爸爸认为短裤的颜色不好，故选C。

[听力原文]

You will hear Paul and his father talking. What does the father think about the shorts?

Son: Dad, look at those shorts for Mum. They're in the sale. I really like them.

Dad: Do you? I'm not sure. They're yellow and black.

Son: What's wrong with yellow and black shorts?

Dad: Your mum doesn't really like those colours.

Son: I think the colours look good. Mum will be happy. Don't worry!

Dad: OK. I'll ask the shop assistant what the sale price is.

20. 根据对话中提到的 "That's a good idea but shoes are going to be expensive.（这是个好主意，但鞋子会很贵。）" 可知，Sally觉得鞋子比较贵，故选C。

[听力原文]

You will hear two friends talking about a birthday. Why aren't shoes a good idea?

A: Sally, what present are you going to buy for your grandmother?

B: She loves jewellery but I bought her earrings last year.

A: What about some shoes or a pair of gloves?

B: That's a good idea but shoes are going to be expensive.

A: I know a shop where there's a good choice of gloves.

B: Great. Can you come with me to buy them?

A: Of course.

Day 5

Test 1

21. F   22. A   23. B   24. C   25. H

[答案详解]

21. 对话中提到 "Peter is coming tomorrow morning to do the garden. The grass is very long so it needs to be cut." 由此可知，Peter要负责打理花园、割草，故选F。

22. 根据对话中的 "And my sister Nikki has offered to clean all the chairs and the tables." 可知，

Nikki主动提出来要打扫所有桌椅，故选A。

23. 根据对话中的 "Emily is organizing the music." 可知，Emily负责音乐，故选B。

24. 根据对话中的 "Lucas will make a big cake." 可知，Lucas会做一个大蛋糕，故选C。

25. 根据 "You know we haven't got a dishwasher, so you can do the washing up!（你知道我们没有洗碗机，所以你可以洗碗！）" 可知，Mike需要洗碗，故选H。

[听力原文]

You will hear two friends talking about a barbecue. What is each person going to do?

Mike: Are you ready for tomorrow's barbecue, Polly?

Polly: No, I'm not. There's still a lot to do. I'm going shopping later to buy the meat, the vegetables and bread.

Mike: Don't forget the sausages. Do you want me to come with you?

Polly: No, it's OK. Everything's under control. My dad is taking me with the car. And (21) Peter is coming tomorrow morning to do the garden. The grass is very long so it needs to be cut. (22) And my sister Nikki has offered to clean all the chairs and the tables. They're very dirty because it's rained a lot.

Mike: Good. What about the music? Do you want me to make a playlist and bring it?

Polly: No, (23) Emily is organizing the music. She's the best.

Mike: I see. Anyway, how about the dessert? Shall I bring some ice cream?

Polly: Oh don't worry, (24) Lucas will make a big cake.

Mike: Mmm… maybe I should buy some ice cream, just in case…

Polly: Don't be silly Mike, Lucas is a wonderful cook! He made some delicious brownies for the end of the year party. I've got a job for you too.

Mike: Good! What do you want me to do?

Polly: (25) You know we haven't got a dishwasher, so you can do the washing up!

Mike: OK. I don't mind.

Test 2

21. B   22. E   23. C   24. G   25. H

[答案详解]

21. 对话中Nora提到可以让Tom带爆米花，但是Fred回复说Tom会买一些软饮和果汁，故选B。

22. 对话中Nora说Isabel可以准备音乐和气球，但是Fred说派对上不需要气球，所以Isabel要准备的就是音乐，故选E。

23. 对话中Nora主动提出可以准备爆米花，故选C。

24. 对话中Fred询问Jason是否会来派对，Nora说Jason会来拍一些照片，故选G。

25. 对话最后，Fred想知道自己要做什么，Nora回复说让Fred买一些比萨，故选H。

[听力原文]

You will hear two friends talking about a party. What will each person help with?

Nora: Hi Fred, is everything ready for the end-of-year party?

Fred: Not really, Nora, there are still a lot of things to do.

Nora: Oh dear. Who is buying the food?

Fred: Well, Yuki will cook the chicken nuggets, but she hasn't got time to prepare the popcorn.

Nora: Maybe Tom can bring the popcorn.

Fred: (21) No, he's going to buy the soft drinks and juices. Let's ask Isabel.

Nora: (22) I think Isabel wanted to bring the music, and the balloons.

Fred: (22) No, there aren't going to be any balloons at the party.

Nora: (23) OK, I can make some popcorn. I haven't got anything to do.

Fred: That's great Nora. Is Jason coming to the party? I haven't seen him for a while.

Nora: Yes, he is. (24) And he's going to take the photographs for the school website.

Fred: That's a good idea. But what am I going to do for the party?

Nora: (25)You should buy some pizza. I think we need some more food.

Fred: You're right. There's never enough food at parties!

小马外语